S U N K E N
TREASURES

THE WORLD'S GREAT SHIPWRECKS

Text
Gaetano Cafiero

Preface
Antonio Soccol

Edited by
Marcello Bertinetti and
Valeria Manferto
  De Fabianis

Designed by
Patrizia Balocco

Illustrations by
Mina Carpi

Thanks are due the following people for their valuable contributions to this book: Luisa Tchabuschnig; Fabio Bourbon; Grazia Neri; Marco Finazzi; Sergio Quaglia; Jorg Keller and Elga Harders from *Tauchen* in Hamburg; E.R. Cross; Ursula Logan; Stuart McLachlan from *Diver* magazine in Teddington, U.K.; Barry Andrewartha from *Sportdiving* magazine in Sidney; and Kendall McDonald, Superintendent of Archeology in Sassary, Italy.

Photo credits appear on page 144.

Published 1993
by Thomasson-Grant

World Copyright © 1992
Edizioni White Star
Via Candido Sassone 22/24
13100 Vercelli, Italy

Title of the original edition:
RELITTI: IMMERSIONI NELLA STORIA

PAGE 1
Cedar Pride, Red Sea.

PAGES 2-3
Wreck of a merchant ship,
Brothers Islands, Red Sea.

PAGE 4-5
Japanese Zero,
Papua New Guinea.

PAGE 6 TOP AND PAGE 7
"K.T.," Sestri Levante,
Mediterranean Sea.

PAGE 6 MIDDLE AND BOTTOM
Gianis D, Red Sea.

Any inquiries should be directed to:
Thomasson-Grant, Inc.,
One Morton Drive, Suite 500
Charlottesville, Virginia
22903-6806
(804)977-1780

Printed in Italy

00 99 98 97 96 95 94 93 5 4 3 2 1

Library of Congress
Cataloging-in-Publication Data
on file

or centuries, navigable bodies of water have been the busy thoroughfares of migration, trade, discovery, military combat, and progress. It is estimated that five percent of all the ships ever to set sail have been wrecked, making the depths of the world's oceans and rivers a veritable museum of man's seafaring history. Shipwrecks give testimony to the immense naval traffic that has been taking place for more than 9,000 years.

The history of navigation precedes even the early papyrus boats of the ancient Egyptians. The first "written" symbol of a ship appears on a clay tablet dating back to the Uruk period in Mesopotamia, 4,000 years before Christ. Unfortunately, none of the ships that sailed before 3200 B.C. has been found, and although no wrecks remain to provide evidence of the fact, there is no doubt that man was a sailor before he was a farmer.

A sunken ship is an irreplaceable record of the civilization of its epoch; it speaks to the level of culture of the people who built it, their ingenuity and skill, and the shipbuilding and other techniques known to them. It gives us information about their trade activity, the routes they sailed, the foods they ate, the clothes and jewelry they wore, the tools and weapons they used, and the religion(s) they observed. A single object found in a wreck can provide scientists and historians with startling new information about the technological sophistication of a particular culture. Consider, for example, the famous "computer" found on the Antikythera wreck. This incredible mechanism, built around 82 B.C. in Rhodes, demonstrates the intricacy with which the ancient Greeks were able to fashion an instrument to predict and track the movement of the major stars and constellations to aid them in navigation. Nothing like the Antikythera computer has been found on any other wreck.

The study of naval wrecks is thus a study of the history of man. Progress in this field was limited until 1942, when Emile Gagnan and Jacques Cousteau developed the aqualung, the first "automatic compressed air respirator for diving"—the prototype of the self-contained underwater breathing apparatus, or scuba. From that moment forward, the study of wrecks received a remarkable boost because the archeologist himself could

actually dive down and be directly involved in the recovery and analysis of important artifacts left unwittingly by our ancestors. At the same time, advances in underwater photography enabled divers to leave wreck sites with clear and definitive documentation of their finds.

Finally, in the last twenty years, more advanced technologies have permitted the building and refinement of research submarines such as *Alvin*, which have made possible the discovery and exploration of wrecks at enormous depths. One such discovery is the *Titanic*, which lies at a depth of more than two-and-a-half miles in the North Atlantic. Compare the extraordinarily gentle touch of the arm of "Robin"— the small, remote-controlled robot of the French submarine *Nautile*, which, at the end of the 1980s, explored the immense *Titanic*—with the clumsy and unwieldy arm of the crane on the *Artiglio II* with which Professor Nino Lamboglia attempted, in the 1950s, to recover the contents of a small Roman ship off Albenga. Previous studies were, of necessity, based only on work at *accessible* sites— half-sunken wrecks or those in shallow waters—

PAGES 10-11
The cargo boat Superior Producer, *sunk in St. Anne Bay, Caribbean Sea, in November 1977.*

PAGES 12-13
Taiwanese fishing boat, Pacific Ocean.

PAGES 14-15
Barracuda swim past a wreck in the Virgin Islands.

and on the abilities of skilled divers working with primitive equipment. In three decades, advances in underwater technology have permitted far more intricate work than ever before in the gathering and examination of samples from wreck sites throughout the world.

An encounter with one of these tragic wrecks inevitably evokes a moment of deep emotion. Every vessel on the sea floor represents an unfinished story, an interrupted journey. But along with the sorrow comes the undeniable attraction of mystery, the irresistible curiosity that so often leads to discoveries that enable us to learn about, and perhaps to mourn, those whose lives the sea has claimed.

Indeed, the story of the discovery of the wreck at Antikythera synthesizes the sequence of emotions man experiences when he comes across a wreck. Elias Stadiatis, who originally discovered the wreck while diving for sponges, fled to the surface terrified, stammering, and overcome by panic, not fully comprehending what he had seen. He reported "a pile of . . . greenish corpses," including horses and naked women, on the sea floor. Dimitrios Kondos, captain of the sponge boat, dove immediately to the bottom and discovered a wealth of bronze statues and other objects in and around what appeared to be an ancient ship. Kondos was elated with the find, and returned to the surface with a bronze arm from one of the statues as proof that Stadiatis had indeed seen "naked bodies." Accounts vary about the sequence of events that followed. Some say that Kondos reported the find to Greek authorities immediately, while others believe that he and his crew removed a considerable portion of the treasure from the wreck before making its presence known.

Those emotions are no less powerful today. Images of the gigantic, rusty anchor of the *Titanic* evoke a shiver of horror, especially when we consider that the ship rests in the dark, cold depths at over 13,000 feet. And the massive tangle of wrecks in the Truk Lagoon inspires awe as we reflect on the hundreds of lives lost when, on February 17, 1944, U.S. forces surprised the Japanese fleet and sank more than sixty of their ships.

We continue to be fascinated by the great work of the sea that takes place on every wreck —at the sight of the brilliant variety of sea life that has taken up residence on a sunken brigantine in the Red Sea, or the "cave" a group of timid conger eels has claimed in a section of the hull of a cargo ship driven against a French cliff by the mistral. And we continue to be in awe of what the world's great shipwrecks have taught us about the shipbuilding and navigational skills of our ancestors.

Antonio Soccol

INTRODUCTION

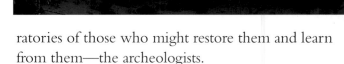

A shipwreck is what remains after a ship goes down—whatever the reason, the time, or the place. A shipwreck is what remains of a means of transport for passengers and their possessions, for commercial cargo, for soldiers and their weapons. The ship may have gone down in an ocean or along a navigable river. It may have run aground, struck an iceberg, been torpedoed, or collided with another ship.

Shipwrecks have different destinies, depending on their age, their contents, their construction, the circumstances under which they sank, and their location. The remains of ancient ships—from Greek and Phoenician ships to eighteenth-century galleons—are primarily of interest to archeologists and marine historians for what they reveal about the era in which they were built. Modern cargo ships that can be reached by experienced diving crews without undue difficulty create business for salvage companies. Passenger ships that are "lost" under thousands of feet of water stimulate costly, often multinational expeditions for which scientists and researchers perfect state-of-the-art submersibles and underwater filming equipment. Near popular vacation spots, ships that rest in shallow waters are exploited by tour operators, who lead groups of amateur divers and even snorklers to visit the wreck site for a fee.

For some, a shipwreck may be significant in yet another way—as a memorial. The Truk Lagoon in Micronesia bears the wreckage of dozens of Japanese ships that were destroyed in a single raid on the fleet during the Second World War. Every year, the lagoon is visited by Japanese who wish to pay tribute to those who lost their lives during that devastating attack.

Unfortunately, for every well-intentioned diver who visits a wreck merely to learn from it, there will be several who are motivated solely by greed, who dive down to the site repeatedly until they have stripped the wreck of everything of value. Those who "feed" upon wrecks in this way have come to be known as *tombaroli*, after the farmers of Lazio and Tuscany who plundered Etruscan tombs they discovered while plowing their fields. These divers are unscrupulous and have little or no appreciation for the historical value of the items they recover; precious objects often end up in the hands of "treasure" brokers and never see the laboratories of those who might restore them and learn from them—the archeologists.

American archeologist George F. Bass once said that underwater archeology does not exist. So curious was I upon hearing this that I sought to purchase his book in 1966, thinking that the title directly contradicted what he was saying. When I acquired the book, I saw that the title was actually *Archaeology Under Water*, and not, as I had originally understood, *Underwater Archaeology*. A reading of the introduction enlightened me as to his choice of title. Dr. Bass wrote: "At recent conferences on underwater archaeology, suggestions have been made for a more attractive title to give this growing new field of research. None is completely suitable. 'Marine' or 'submarine' archaeology would limit the work to that done in the seas, while much has been done in rivers, lakes, and wells; 'hydroarchaeology' could include the study of ancient sources of water; and the hybrid 'aquaeology' is no closer to being an adequate title. Archaeology under water, of course, should be called simply archaeology. We do not speak of those working on top of Nimrud Dagh in Turkey as mountain archaeologists, nor those at Tikal in Guatemala as jungle archaeologists. They are all people who are trying to answer questions regarding man's past, and they are adaptable in being able to excavate and interpret ancient buildings, tombs, and even entire cities with the artifacts which they contain. Is the study of an ancient ship and its cargo, or the survey of toppled harbour walls somehow different? That such remains may lie under water entails the use of different tools and techniques in their study, just as the survey of a large area on land, using aerial photographs, magnetic detectors, and drills, requires a procedure other than excavating the stone artifacts and bones in a Palaeolithic cave. The basic aim in all these cases is the same. It is all archaeology." (George F. Bass, *Archaeology Under Water*, Frederick A. Praeger, 1966.) One cannot be indifferent to the arguments of Dr. Bass. But the fact remains that the term "underwater archeology" is accepted worldwide.

An archeologist who has scientific interest in all that lies under water must be a good diver. If not, he should at least be able to rely on assistants and collaborators, themselves archeologists, who are. An archeologist who is in charge of an excava-

PAGE 16

Cedar Pride, *Red Sea.*

PAGE 17

Yongala, *Great Barrier Reef.*

tion campaign is responsible for all work done by his staff, and he must survey the work step by step. He must be able to organize and direct all phases of the recovery of materials found at the underwater site. George F. Bass is a well-known scholar. He is also an able diver.

And so is Miss Honor Frost, an elderly and cheerful English lady, who, while diving near Sicily, surprisingly came upon a Phoenician warship. Elisha Linder, another scholar and diver, found the intact rostrum of a Roman warship near Haifa. Many other scholars and scientists are capable divers: Meneun Bound, an Englishman born in the Falklands, director of archeology at MARI Maritime Archaeological Research Institute of Oxford University, author of important research on an Etruscan wreck near Giglio Island and a Greek wreck near Panarea Island; Claudio Mocchegiani Carpano of STAS, the technical service of the underwater archeology program of the Ministry of Cultural Properties in Italy; and Luigi Fozzati, who works for the same public body and also for the archeological branch of Turin University. All are well-known scholars responsible for projects of great scientific interest; they have all become "archeologists under water"— whether because, when children, they dove and followed fish between the rocks, or, as adult divers, came upon an amphora (there are millions of them along the Mediterranean coast). They are all scientists who welcome the collaboration of colleagues who are beginners and often guide them to enhance their understanding of a given discovery.

Archeology is a multidisciplinary science, underwater archeology even more so, for obvious reasons. During the recovery of a wreck that has been submerged for hundreds or even thousands of years, the various pieces of the wreck must be removed with great care so that they may be studied, reassembled, preserved, and exhibited in a museum; this is the ultimate goal of any archeological campaign. These activities require the collaboration of chemists, physicians, oceanologists, oceanographical engineers, nautical architects, photographers, designers, and laboratory technicians. Many of them participate in the process not for financial reward but for the pleasure of contributing to the process of restoring and learning from a relic that has come from the sea that they love so much.

The wrecks among the Red Sea coral reefs are spectacular sights for divers, with the extraordinary variety of the thousands of sea organisms that inhabit these waters. But it must not be forgotten that the sinking of a ship is always a terrible disaster that often claims many lives and proves a great loss to the country under whose flag the ship was sailing.

PAGES 18, 19
Cedar Pride, *Red Sea.*

This book is about wrecks and those who study them. Perhaps it would be more precise, then, when speaking about archeology that deals with sunken ships, to call it naval archeology. It is not limited to "under water" since it is practised even on ancient ships found on the mainland. For example, there are the ships that were buried in the Egyptian desert—alongside the pyramids and the tombs of the pharaohs and other dignitaries—so that they could carry the deceased to the Reign of the Dead, and, similarly, there are the "ship graves" of the Vikings.

For those who wish to pursue naval archeology but lack experience as divers, the Professional Association of Diving Instructors (PADI) offers official certification as a "wreck diver" to those who complete a special course organized by the association. Exploring a wreck is not an easy task for the amateur diver. Merely the touch of an inexperienced diver can cause great damage to structures that time and water have made very fragile. When a ship has been under water for one or two centuries, the diver who approaches it exposes himself to great risk: a sudden yielding can cause the wreck to give way, collapsing on the diver or blocking the opening through which he entered, leaving him with no means of escape.

In contrast to vestigial ancient vessels, the wrecks of modern ships sunk in tropical waters offer thrilling underwater adventures and spectacular photographic opportunities. The solid metal structures make excellent homes for the many species of marine creatures that inhabit those waters. The wrecks blossom with corals and sponges, and the smooth steel is covered over with the thousands of different forms of life that occupy every inch of a ship's outer surface. In a splendid metamorphosis, the sea and its creatures take possession of an inanimate work of man, embrace it, and change it into a magnificent ecosystem.

The glamour of exploring a wreck lies in the quality and history of the things a diver finds. While diving with air tanks on his back and the demand apparatus between his teeth, he may come across an amphora, a lantern, a gold or bronze coin, or a bronze statue and feel a sudden rush of adrenalin. Occasionally, an underwater "find" will come from an entirely different source than the shipwreck that

TOP

The Giglio Island wreck was accidentally discovered by amateur divers exploring the waters near the port. Archeological researchers in Florence concluded that it was a Roman cargo ship that probably sank because of a fire on board.

BOTTOM

The Cape Coda Cavallo wreck is a Roman munitions ship of the third century A.D.

happens to be nearby. For example, it is probable that the two bronzes of Riace found by Stefano Mariottini were not part of the cargo of a Roman ship wrecked along the coast of Calabria, nearby, but were thrown overboard from a passing cargo ship that ran into a terrible storm. Some maintain that the two statues were accidentally dredged up in the Adriatic by fishermen, who, when they realized the difficulties of transporting the bronze masses back to the harbor, decided to throw them into the Tyrrhenian Sea.

My first personal archeological find was a perfect, intact amphora, its clay stopper still in place, sealed with pine resin. We carefully removed the stopper and dared to taste the twenty-centuries-old wine. I also remember exploring an English cargo vessel, the *M.V. Kent*, wrecked near San Vito Lo Capo, Sicily: it carried insecticides, polystyrene bags, and, in four containers, thousands of copies of the Koran from the sixteenth century. I recovered a badly burned copy, took it with me, and laid it out to dry in the sun. After a few days, it was beautiful. I kept it in a transparent box.

And finally, I remember the *Yongala*, wrecked in March of 1911 off Townsville, Queensland, Australia. I was taken there by a yacht skipper with a peg leg (he seemed a pirate). The yacht had been chartered by a group who wanted to film a documentary on the reproduction of corals. The skipper explained that the wreck site had not been marked, in an attempt to discourage plunderers. I asked how we would know when to jump into the water. "When you see the water snakes that come to the surface to breathe and the fins of the sharks that swim around, that is the right place. Jump in the middle and sink," he answered.

We obeyed. Snakes and sharks squirted away, terrified. We sank obliquely, carried along by a strong current, and crossed a deep cloud of thousands of batfish and a forest of silver "ferns"— colonies of hydroids. Ninety-eight feet down, along the side of the overturned stern, we were welcomed by a school of enormous sea bass, which despite their large size, were very friendly and affectionate.

Gaetano Cafiero

TOP

The wreck of the galleon Grand Saint-Antoine, *near Marseille, dates to 1720.*

BOTTOM

The wreck of the Aber Wrac'h, *discovered in 1985 along the French coast, dates back to the first half of the fifteenth century. Research indi-* *cates it was probably an English cargo boat belonging to Sir Richard Barquier. It sank in 1435 not far from the mouth of the Aber River.*

SUNKEN TREASURES

NORTH AMERICA

THE TITANIC (1912)

THE ANDREA DORIA (1956)

THE CENTRAL AMERICA (1857)

THE ATOCHA (1622)

THE TAMAYA (1902)

THE CONDE DE TOLOSA (1724)

TRUK LAGOON (1944)

THE PACIFIC THEATER

THE BATAVIA (1629)

THE PRESIDENT COOLIDGE (1942)

AUSTRALIA

THE EMDEN (1914)

THE YONGALA (1911)

ATLANTIC OCEAN

THE ROYAL OAK (1919)

THE GIRONA (1588)

EUROPE

ANCIENT ROMAN WRECKS
(FIRST CENTURY B.C.)

THE HAVEN (1991)

THE RUBIS (1957)

THE "K.T." (1944)

VILLEFRANCHE (1500-1520)

THE FLYING FORTRESS (1943)

CAPE GELIDONYA
(1300-1100 B.C.)

SERÇE LIMANI (1100-1200)

AFRICA

SEA OF GALILEE
(500-400 B.C.)

THE CARNATIC (1869)

CONSHELF TWO (1963)

THE RED SEA

THE UMBRIA (1940)

N

THE MERCHANTS OF THE BRONZE AGE

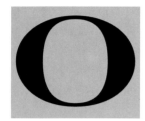

On a summer day in 1959 a group of sponge divers from Bodrum was working at a depth of about ninety feet near Cape Gelidonya ("Cape of the Swallows") off the southern coast of Turkey. They came across some old copper ingots, which they later described to a friend as being plentiful at that site. The friend, Peter Throckmorton, soon understood what they had seen—"ox-hide" ingots that led him to discover the oldest known shipwreck, dating back to the Bronze Age.

Throckmorton quickly organized an expedition to excavate the site, serving as technical adviser. He invited a young research assistant from the University of Pennsylvania Museum—George F. Bass—to be director. Bass, who had never donned a wet suit, hastily took a diving course at the YMCA; when he plunged into the water at Cape Gelidonya, it was his first sea dive.

The largest pieces of cargo were indeed copper ingots, most of which were covered by lime deposits. Forty of these were the so-called "ox-hide" or "four-handled" ingots. Among other items recovered were bronze tools, amphorae, scale weights, a Syrian scarab, and agricultural implements. From the artifacts removed from the wreck, researchers concluded that the ship sailed around 1200 B.C., carrying a load of copper from the mines in Cyprus. It is not known, however, whether the ship was Syrian, Cyprian, or Greek. (Remarkably, the ship matched the description of a ship built by Odysseus.) Neither the cargo nor the wood from which the ship was constructed provided conclusive evidence of the ship's national origin.

The recovered objects, wood fragments, and thorough scientific studies allowed researchers to draw from this authentic time capsule—hidden under water for more than 3,000 years—a rich harvest of information about the life, the trade routes, and the international relationships of the people in the Mediterranean at the extreme edge of history. The finds confirmed what was believed to be true up to that time, thanks to the Homeric poems, whose protagonists lived, loved, and fought in the places touched by the nameless ship. The ship that lies in shallow waters at the Cape of the Swallows was occupied by unlucky sailors, who probably died during a storm in an expanse of that small sea that held the entire known world.

The discovery of the ship at Gelidonya, sunk over 3,000 years ago, is of extraordinary historical value. Shown above is a sampling of the ingots and small amphorae found on the wreck. (Facing) Divers recover an intact amphora. (Overleaf) Divers carefully catalog each item recovered from the wreck site.

Among the many handmade items recovered from the wreck at Cape Gelidonya are weapons, several scarabs, pitchers, lamps, and amphorae. Divers even found the bottom of a rope basket—preserved, remarkably, after over 3,000 years under water. It is believed that the cape lay along a shipping route for copper and bronze traders in the Late Bronze Age. The largest portion of the ship's cargo consisted of copper ingots.

THE WRECK NEAR THE KIBBUTZ

lisha Linder is a sabra (a native-born Israeli) living on the Ma'agan Michael kibbutz in Caesarea. A world-famous archeologist, he is head of the Institute for Marine Studies at the University of Haifa and is a member of the Israel Underwater Exploration Society. He has skillfully led important expeditions at Caesarea, Akko, and Atlit along the Israeli coast. In 1986, two brothers from the kibbutz discovered the remains of an ancient ship in the Sea of Galilee. The brothers had been swimming with mask and flippers along the shoreline, when they came upon several huge basalt blocks in the seabed at a depth of about six feet. Thinking it odd for them to be in that environment, they quickly informed Shelley Wachsmann of the Department of Antiquities and Museums, of the find (Linder was in Sardinia at the time). Wachsmann immediately engaged all divers in the kibbutz in an exploration of the site. Beneath the sand and those blocks of basalt was the wreck of an ancient ship. After a preliminary investigation of the site, the research was granted to Elisha Linder and Avner Raban, assisted by Jay Rosloff of Texas A & M University.

Linder soon organized a team of professional underwater archeologists and directed the expedition. Sir Anthony Jacobs, a Londoner, offered to cover all expenses. The first excavation campaign lasted from October 10 to December 5, 1988. Since the wreck was situated in very deep waters, the slightest wave could compromise the work of the divers. To circumvent this, workers dug a horseshoe trench around the wreck and built a wall of 1,350 sacks of sand around the perimeter. In this way, the sand on the sea floor, as it was shifted by the waves, was prevented from entering and covering over the excavation site.

The basalt structures proved to be the ballast of the ship. It is almost certain the ship was launched in the fifth century B.C. "I was standing on the beach, classifying the finds as they were brought to me. And little by little I understood that we were in the presence of a discovery of great scientific importance," Linder said. During the first excavation season, more than half a ton of the ballast blocks that had attracted the discoverer's attention were removed—only a third of the entire amount. It was a pleasant surprise to the archeolo-

gists to notice that most of the small objects recovered were intact and in excellent condition—baked clay handmade articles including a pot, a great number of jugs and bottles, drinking cups, and lamps. There were wrought metals, including a quantity of iron nails and a device that seemed to be an incense burner. Among the stones a kind of anvil was found. The remains of organic materials were identified as board planks, hay bales probably employed to separate the lumber from the ballast, a basket, ropes, tools, pieces of furniture, and remnants of food.

Studies carried out on fragments of the wood employed to build the hull allowed Jay Rosloff to make important discoveries. What struck him in particular was the wide employment of iron nails to fix the planking to the frame: in the fifth century B.C. (and even at the beginning of the fourth—the period of the wreck as established through an examination by Michael Artzv of the pottery), iron was a precious mineral and only during the Middle Ages would it have known widespread use in naval construction in the Mediterranean.

The Sea of Galilee ship is most likely a Phoenician merchant ship, and it carried a cargo that reflected Mediterranean navigational routes during the historical period dominated by Carthage and Persia. According to Rosloff, the "J"-shaped wooden anchor, beautifully preserved under the sand for 2,400 years, is unique. When Elisha Linder ultimately decided, after three intense underwater excavation campaigns, to raise the wreck to the surface, a marvelous and magnificently preserved keel was brought to light. It was cut from of a single oak log, some thirty-six feet long from stem to stern, clearly marked by the step of the mast.

"In the end," Linder concluded, "I realized that reality had exceeded my most fanciful dreams: what we brought to light, a complete hull from prow to stern, will be a milestone in further research about ships and navigation in ancient times and in understanding the system of relationships that exist between man and the sea."

Just off the coastline near Ma'agan Michael kibbutz in Caesarea, Israeli archeologists discovered the wreck of an ancient ship. Discoveries such as this enable archeologists to reconstruct details of the seafaring life of our remote ancestors. In ancient times, the small ships that sailed in the Mediterranean did most of their trading along the coastline; they were not equipped with instruments that would enable them to undertake long voyages across open sea. For this reason, most of the ships were sunk in shallow waters, within easy reach of modern-day divers and archeologists.

Scientists and archeologists use state-of-the-art equipment to explore the ancient wreck—presumed to be a Phoenician merchant ship. The unique wooden anchor is remarkably well preserved. The ship was raised to the surface after three excavation campaigns; the hull was complete from prow to stern.

THE ROUTE OF THE ANCIENT ROMANS

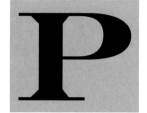

Practically speaking, the wreck found at Albenga marked the birth of modern underwater archeology. It carried a cargo of 10,000 amphorae of wine from Campania bound for the markets of southern Gaul and Hyberia. It was discovered by a fisherman from Albenga—Antonio Bignone—in 1933. But it was not until 1950 that an official expedition was organized to explore the wreck; it was to be led by archeologist Nino Lamboglia, director of the Institute of Ligurian Studies. The aqualung had not yet been invented, and Professor Lamboglia, for the first "excavation" campaign, made use of the divers and the technical equipment of the legendary *Artiglio II*, which had recovered a cargo of gold ingots from the *Egypt*, sunk at a depth of 396 feet in the Bay of Biscay, eighteen years earlier. The owner of the salvage company, Commandatore Giovanni Quaglia, put his equipment at Lamboglia's disposal.

A great deal of interesting material was recovered, but much damage was done by the steel "grab" of the *Artiglio II*, the only instrument available for digging down into the soft mud. The grab was far too crude to retrieve the fragile amphorae without breaking them, and each "bite" stirred up so much mud that divers could not see clearly for hours. Lamboglia quickly realized that the delicate artifacts of a wreck must be carefully removed by a team of professional salvage divers; the wreck at Albenga was an ideal starting point for underwater archeology.

Another Roman wreck can be found off the tiny island of Mal di Ventre, just south of Cape Mannu in Sardinia. Following the discovery of the wreck by diver Antonello Atzori in 1988, archeologists concentrated their attention on the central part of the ship, which contained a large quantity of lead ingots. The wreck was that of a Roman munitions ship, and the lead had been extracted from a mine worked twenty centuries ago. By the end of 1991, the third excavation campaign, under the supervision of the Archeology Office for the provinces of Cagliari and Oristano, came to an end. The weight of the ingots and the names imprinted on the surface enabled archeologists to determine that the wreck dated back to the first century B.C. Many of the 900 ingots recovered bore the trademark of the Pon-

tileni family—presumably the owners of the mine and the foundry, whose lead ingots had already been found in other parts of the Mediterranean.

The ship probably remained horizontal as it sank. As it approached the seabed, it struck a rock in the sediments and heeled on its left side, coming to rest with the stern slightly raised. On examining the keel, the planking, and the frames, researchers surmised that these parts of the ship were saved from destruction by sea organisms and by the large number of lead ingots present, which had in some way insulated the wood from the underwater surroundings.

At a depth of 1,500 feet, in the waters off Diano Marina, near western Liguria, lies another ship—a contemporary of the Mal di Ventre wreck. It is "the ship of the jars"—a forerunner of the modern-day tanker—discovered in 1975. The Latin name for the jars such as those found on the wreck at Diano Marina is *dolia*. They are huge terracotta amphorae, each with a capacity of from 300 to 700 gallons. From the Diano Marina wreck, fourteen have been recovered to date, together with three smaller ones, called *doliola*. When archeologists were able to examine it, they established that the ship is one of the most important wrecks of the Roman period to be discovered along the coast of Liguria and one of the most important in the Mediterranean.

The enormous terracotta jars found on the ancient wreck at Diano Marina were comparable to the tanks of modern cargo vessels built purposely for the transport of liquids. These ancient ships were actually assembled after the great amphorae had been put into position on the bottom planking and on the keel—a construction technique that differed significantly from that used on smaller ships carrying smaller amphorae, which were loaded into the hold after construction was complete.

The discovery of centuries-old ships such as the one (shown at right) found near Giens, France, has enabled historians to reconstruct the routes followed by trading ships of that time and to learn about the cargos they carried and the ways in which their ships were constructed.

The discovery of the wreck at Albenga (above) marked the birth of modern underwater archeology. Discovered by a fisherman in 1933, the ship was carrying thousands of amphorae of wine. Early recovery efforts were conducted from the Artiglio II, but many of the items were damaged in the process. A later expedition involved an archeologist, who supervised a thorough and careful excavation and photographic survey. "Archeology under water," as George F. Bass would call it later, had been born. Pictured at right are lead ingots on the wreck at Mal di Ventre.

THE GLASS WRECK

Serçe Limani, "Sparrow Harbor" in Turkish, is a little cove that opens out onto the Turkish coast of the Aegean Sea, north of the island of Rhodes. The nearest cities are Bodrum and Marmaris. Around these ports an endless number of wrecks are hidden by the sea. In the summer of 1974, George F. Bass was led by a retired sponge diver named Mehmet Askin to a place where "there [was] glass everywhere down below." But Bass had a cold and was unable to dive with his friend Yüksel Edgemir, a commissioner of Turkey's Department of Antiquities. After examining the amphorae Edgemir recovered that day, Bass estimated their date in the twelfth or thirteenth century.

Although Bass was busy concluding research he'd begun on other wrecks, Serçe Limani remained in his mind. In the spring of 1977, he decided to explore the site where Mehmet had found "glass everywhere" in hopes of finding a wreck. By June he was ready to depart from Bodrum, heading up a team of twenty American and Turkish divers. Bass described the expedition in an article for the June 1978 issue of *National Geographic* magazine: "Within the space of a few weeks, we collected whole specimens or fragments of nearly 200 different forms and shapes of glassware. The range and beauty of their colors dazzled us."

As more and more objects were recovered from the wreck, members of the team grew closer to an accurate dating of the ship. Finally, a group of badly eroded copper coins provided sufficient evidence to place the ship in the early eleventh century. Determining the ship's origin proved to be much more difficult. Certain items were clearly Islamic, while others were Greek. The port of origin of the glass wreck is still unknown.

By the end of the summer, Bass's team had recovered a huge collection of glassware, amphorae, and other artifacts for the museum at Bodrum. But perhaps their greatest find was the ship itself—it was like no other they had seen. Unlike the early Greek and Roman ships, which were built without an inner framework, this vessel's hull planking was built on a skeleton of keel and ribs. Excavators on the Bass team felt that they may have come upon one of the earliest known "modern" ships.

Although the season's work on a wreck filled with broken glass was fraught with obvious dangers (none of the divers wore gloves), it proved to be extremely rewarding; team members could not wait to see what they would find from one day to the next. The exhilaration of exploring the wreck in spite of the hazards involved is best described by Bass himself: "Each time my diving partners or I cut a hand or finger while exploring the bottom of that small harbor on the Aegean Sea, we were rewarded with another masterpiece of the ancient glassworker's art. More important still, we were rewarded with priceless new knowledge of man's early attempts to conquer the sea."

Maritime traffic resumed in the eleventh century after the Saracen pirates were driven out of their base in the Mediterranean. The ships of the Italian maritime republics were free to sail the waters near their homeland once again. The Byzantines ensured the control of the Aegean Sea and its surrounding territories for themselves. Their galleys, equipped with sails and oars, sailed for Constantinople from Venice. The glass wreck dates back to this historical period.

Researchers believe that the cargo of the ship found at Serçe Limani was largely glass. Among the items recovered from the wreck were this tumbler (left) with engraved Picasso-like lions and this bottle (right) with a design engraved by a grinding wheel. According to George F. Bass, whose diving team recovered the cargo in 1977, the bottle "represents the finest of the ship's glass . . . . In a technique still used today, some manganese was added to the molten glass to render it clear as crystal and free of color."

In a meticulous system of organization for the excavation work done on the wreck, Bass's team set up a metal grid that enabled divers to determine the exact location of each object recovered. This scientific method, combined with the skill of the divers, made it possible for the team to recover and catalog thousands of fragments of worked glass, many undamaged pieces, glass balance-scale weights, Byzantine coins, a sword hilt, earthenware items, millstones, lead fishing sinkers, and the anchors of the ship. The coins enabled scientists to date the ship back to the early eleventh century, but it is still not known whether the ship is Greek or Islamic.

A Sixteenth-Century Mystery

Although several archeological and research expeditions have been conducted on the wreck at Ville-franche, little is known about the ship. It sank in the early sixteenth century and is believed to have come from Genoa.

illefranche is located on the southeastern tip of France, between Nice and Monte Carlo. Not more than a third of a mile from the shore at Villefranche, at a depth of about sixty feet, lies the wreck of an armored ship, probably from Genoa, that sank between 1500 and 1520. It was discovered in 1979 by Alain Visquis, owner of a firm that specializes in underwater work. In spite of numerous archeological and research expeditions that have been carried out, not much is really known about this ship. The longitudinal axis of the wreck is oriented in a north-south direction. A good bit of the starboard and keel planking of the floor timbers and frames is still well preserved, and the remains of the main and lower decks are well visible. The destructive action of the teredo worm has been observed on the wood. The bottom planking of the Villefranche vessel was covered with lead sheets, like some of the more ancient hulls.

The recovery of the lower part of the helm, and the fact that the keel, from the junction point with the sternpost, had been cut from a single block of wood about twenty-three feet long and thirty-one inches high, were of great interest to researchers. When the ship was plowing through the sea, it had to have a maximum length of between 120 and 160 feet, the maximum beam (i.e., the width) had to be thirty-six feet, while the height to the main deck has been calculated at approximately fifteen feet.

A heap of large stone cannonballs was found in the middle of the ship, along with two cart wheels, an iron cannon, and a wooden winch. The material recovered from the ship is quite varied: besides cannons and their ammunition, lead shot for a harquebus (a fifteenth-century gun) and a culverin (a type of musket), and double-press forging dies to manufacture them on board, there were swords with their scabbards, several buckles, lead fishing weights, bottles, and coins. There was also decorative pottery from Genoa and Tuscany. In many tiny jars researchers found traces of Greek gunpowder, as if the containers had been used as grenades to defend the ship against a forced boarding.

An air of mystery surrounds the wreck discovered near Villefranche. From the construction, researchers have speculated that the ship was Italian, and from the cargo, that it was an armored ship. The wreck site has been transformed into an underwater laboratory, complete with air lifts, wire grids, weighted measuring tapes, and every conceivable excavation tool, as recovery operations proceed with the hope of providing answers to questions about the ship's origin, route, passengers, and destination. Objects recovered to date, in addition to weapons, include plates, terracotta vases, decorative pottery, and coins.

A GALLEASS OF THE ARMADA

The story of the *Girona* and its discovery in the waters near Northern Ireland is the story of the "invincible" Spanish Armada and its defeat. The *Girona* was one of the four galleasses of the Neapolitan fleet under the command of Don Alonso Martinez de Leiva. Each of these formidable war machines housed a total of 1,300 men, between oarsmen, soldiers, and able seamen.

The Spanish Armada was assembled by Philip II of Spain in 1586. At the end of May 1588, the Armada left Lisbon; it was composed of sixty-five galleons and armed merchantmen, twenty-five transport ships loaded with horses, mules, and supplies, thirty-two small sailing craft, the four Neapolitan galleasses, and four Portuguese galleys. Collectively, they were armed with 2,400 pieces of ordnance and had on board 27,500 soldiers; there were also sailors, convicts, galley slaves, and a small group of wealthy gentlemen.

The first victims of wind and currents were the four Portuguese galleys. Then, the *Girona*— the flagship of the galleasses—struck a submerged rock on October 26, 1588, at Lacada Point off Northern Ireland, and all but five of the men on board drowned. Four centuries later, Robert Stenuit, a Belgian, found the *Girona* off the coast of Belfast.

A total of 6,000 hours of work on the seabed were necessary to put the pieces of the hull and its contents together. By the time the expedition had ended, divers had recovered an anchor, compasses, an astrolabe, silver and tin plates, candelabra, gold, silver, and copper pieces from Spain, Naples, Portugal, Genoa, Mexico, and Peru, a reliquary, a cross of the Knights of Malta, an Alcántara knight's medallion, silver crucifixes, gold jacket buttons, jewels, gold chains, gold rings, and lapis lazuli cameos framed in gold and set with pearls. The *Girona* yielded the greatest finds of all the Armada relics.

Belgian scuba diver Robert Stenuit described his feelings about the spectacular find of the Girona after years of exhausting research—four centuries after the ship went down. "For me the wreck of the Girona is a concentration of history, of tragedy, of treasure, and finding it became an obsession, my reason for living."

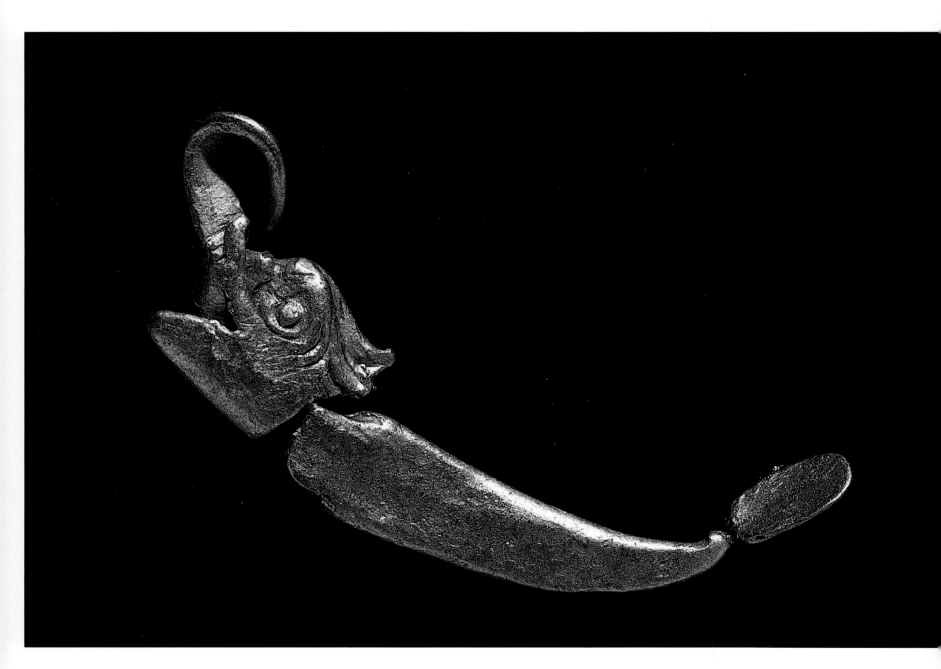

Designed and built for coastal
trade in the Mediterranean, the
Girona *was the flagship galleass
of the Neapolitan fleet and part
of the Spanish Armada. The
ship struck a rock during a wild
north wind, killing all but five of
the 1,300 men on board. Thou-*
sands of hours of work on the
wreck have yielded a number of
exquisite examples of the ship's
rich cargo—including gold, silver,
and copper coins, gold chains,
ornate jewelry, crucifixes, and
candelabra.

A Reef of
Silver Bars

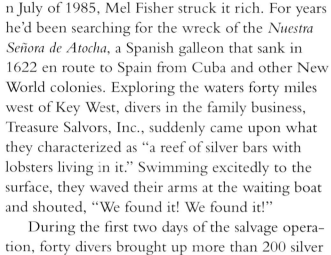

In July of 1985, Mel Fisher struck it rich. For years he'd been searching for the wreck of the *Nuestra Señora de Atocha*, a Spanish galleon that sank in 1622 en route to Spain from Cuba and other New World colonies. Exploring the waters forty miles west of Key West, divers in the family business, Treasure Salvors, Inc., suddenly came upon what they characterized as "a reef of silver bars with lobsters living in it." Swimming excitedly to the surface, they waved their arms at the waiting boat and shouted, "We found it! We found it!"

During the first two days of the salvage operation, forty divers brought up more than 200 silver ingots weighing a total of seven tons. Each bar was fifteen inches long and weighed about seventy pounds. One diver described the scene below in this way: "The silver was stacked up like cordwood as far as the eye could see." In order to protect his find, Fisher ordered a ring of seven salvage ships to stand watch over the site. More than eighty investors had contributed to the salvage expedition, and Fisher wanted to guarantee that their faith in him would be rewarded.

A lengthy legal battle ensued between Fisher, the state of Florida, and the federal government over ownership of the *Atocha*'s cargo. The Supreme Court ruled in favor of Fisher's claim to the treasure. Fisher and his family were amply paid for their patience and hard work, and his financial backers of Treasure Salvors, Inc. received a handsome return on their investments.

The *Atocha* was a heavily armed warship of the Spanish *Tierra Firme* fleet that carried consignments of royal treasure from various ports in the Spanish colonies. The fleet set sail from Cartagena (the stop after Portobello) on July 27 and arrived in Havana on August 22. There, the bulk of the fleet's treasure was divided between the *Atocha* and her sister ship, the *Santa Margarita*. Fitted with twenty bronze cannons, the *Atocha* served as a guard ship for the fleet, which departed from Havana on September 4.

On the second day of the journey, the fleet was rocked by a hurricane; twenty of the twenty-eight vessels managed to escape the violent winds and rolling seas and sail to safety. The *Atocha* was thrown against the reefs along the Florida keys and sank almost immediately; 260 of the 265 persons

The wrecks of the Spanish ships Nuestra Señora de Atocha *and* Santa Margarita *were regarded as underwater gold and silver mines. (The* Santa Margarita *is pictured on the right.) But it took Mel Fisher's team years of exploring, with input from maritime historians and geographers along the way, to locate the "mother lode"—the fabulous treasure of the* Atocha. *Above, Fisher's team celebrates the discovery.*

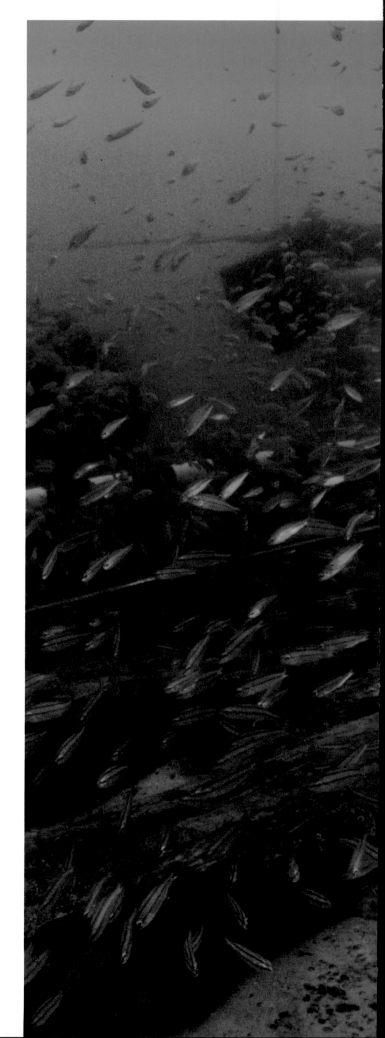

Pictured here is a small sampling of the gold coins, chains, and emeralds found on the Atocha. *In addition to the recovery of the immense treasure from the two famous seventeenth-century*

Spanish galleons, Mel Fisher sought to make a contribution to science and added archeologists to his team, who mapped the site and catalogued the artifacts.

on board drowned. The *Margarita* suffered a similar fate. Millions of dollars of treasure went down with the two ships—a devastating loss for the royal treasury. The wrecks were left undisturbed for centuries—until Mel Fisher began his relentless search for the king's missing treasure.

He founded Treasure Salvors, Inc. in 1969. The company had not had an easy time searching for the three-masted galleon. Discoveries of pieces of treasure had been almost constant, but time and time again, these finds proved to be only "scattered treasure" and not indications that they had found the actual wreck site.

Mel Fisher displayed some of the jewels and coins recovered from the seabed in his shop in Key West; he hoped that the glitter of gold and silver would attract people willing to finance the recovery enterprise. In the end, many people believed in Fisher's dream—several hundred shareholders individually purchased 1,000-dollar shares. And there were professional investors who contributed millions of dollars to the operation.

The scuba divers of Treasure Salvors, Inc. had discovered and salvaged treasure from the *Santa Margarita* in 1980. Among the treasure recovered were forty-three gold chains, each with handmade links. The *Santa Margarita* became known as the "Gold Chain Wreck."

Five years earlier, Dirk Fisher, Mel's son, had found three silver ingots and one of the anchors of the *Atocha* in an area called "Quicksands." He continued to search in the same area, convinced he had located the wreck. Tragically, he drowned, together with his wife and another scuba diver, one night when the rough sea and the wind capsized his small boat. He did not know that the treasure he sought was lying seven miles away, scattered by the violence of the hurricane that had sunk the galleon 351 years earlier.

In 1973, Mel Fisher added an archeologist to his team, hoping to contribute invaluable information to the literature of marine archeology. While many archeologists firmly believe that the interests of treasure salvors and underwater archeologists are completely at odds, the fact remains that the wreck sites of the *Atocha* and the *Santa Margarita* yielded significant information about the seventeenth-century "treasure fleet."

The discovery of the wreck of the *Nuestra Seño-ra de Atocha* permitted Mel Fisher and his enthusiastic backers to undertake new expeditions. Numerous galleons loaded with treasure had sunk during the period of European colonization. Fisher even thought of recovering the treasure of the *San José*, sunk sixteen miles off the coast of Colombia on May 28, 1708, in an attack by the English fleet. Lost that day with the *San José* were the Spanish captain, José Fernandez de Santillan, 600 people, and a load of gold and silver ingots, doubloons, and jewels even more precious than the treasure of the *Atocha*. The *San José* settled on the floor of the Pacific at a depth of 750 feet. In 1983 her treasure was estimated at a billion dollars. But traditional divers cannot work at such depths; only extreme-depth divers can explore these ships. In addition, the government of Colombia let it clearly be known that, because the wreck is lying within its territorial waters, "adventurous treasure hunters" would not be allowed to have access to it.

These gold bars, found on the Atocha, are clearly marked with stamps and seals that indicate the mint where they were cast, the purity of the bar, and other information that enabled them to be dated.

THE *BATAVIA*

MASSACRE IN THE HOUTMAN ABROLHOS

The Dutch East India Company ship *Batavia* has been among the most famous wrecks in the world for almost four centuries. She split apart on the night of June 4, 1629—having struck a reef off an island of the Houtman Abrolhos archipelago in the Indian Ocean near western Australia. The wreck of the *Batavia* set the stage for one of the bloodiest tragedies in seafaring history. It remains the symbol of an Australian geographical anomaly, and marks the first consistent trail left by Europeans on Australian territory.

The few small islands off which the *Batavia* went down were discovered in 1619 by Frederick de Houtman, commander of the *Dordrecht* and a Dutch naval squadron sent to explore the southern seas. To the name Houtman (after the commander), the Portuguese, possibly the best navigators of all time, added a second name for the islands—Abrolhos (from *abre os olhos,* "keep your eyes open"), meant to serve as a warning to sailors to beware of the coral reef that, in truth, should not even be there. In fact, the islands are located at a latitude too high for the ocean water to be sufficiently warm to ensure conditions for the formation of coral reefs. The formation is precipitated by the equatorial Leeuwin Current (named after another ship in the Houtman Squadron), which creates an ecological environment that fosters the accumulation of madrepores. The fish found in the area help mark the border between tropical and temperate waters; coral reef fish are found together with fish typically seen in waters at the higher latitudes.

The adventure of the *Batavia* began in October 1628, when the ship, commanded by Ariaen Jocobsz, left Amsterdam on its maiden voyage. The *Batavia* was the flagship of a fleet of three vessels, and Francisco Pelsaert, president of the fleet, was on board. The ship's hold had been loaded with the usual trade and supply merchandise—fabric, cochineal, wine, and cheese—and twelve chests of silver coins for the purchase of goods in the Indies. A fabulous array of jewels, including a cameo made by the painter Rubens, was tucked away in the captain's cabin. During the voyage, second officer Jeronimus Cornelisz led an unsuccessful attempt to take over the ship and its cargo and use it for pirating activities.

During the night of June 4, 1629, the helmsman steered the ship directly toward the coral reef surrounding the islands in the Houtman Abrolhos archipelago; the watchman assured him that the white foam he saw dead ahead was nothing more than the reflection of the moon on the water. When the ship struck the reef, soundings were taken all around; the depth at the stern was twenty-six feet and much less at the bow. The ship split open and flooded but remained on the reef. In order to lighten the ship, the crew cut the main mast at its base and tossed the bow gun into the sea.

The following morning a lifeboat was sent ashore to explore the small islands nearby and to locate a suitable place for the accomodation of the passengers. Of the 250 people who tried to swim ashore, forty drowned. Then, with the women, children, and injured survivors safely on shore, Pelsaert and Jacobsz decided to leave to get help. With Pelsaert away, Jeronimus Cornelisz became the leader of the survivors and decided to pursue his original plan—when the relief ship arrived he would capture it and use it for piracy. To do this, he first had to do away with the crew members who were not loyal to him.

The shipwreck survivors—passengers and crew—had settled in as well as they could on three islands: Traitors' Island—so-called after Pelsaert left; Batavia's Graveyard, where most of the men and women as well as Cornelisz had come ashore; and a third, unnamed island, to which a group of forty-five soldiers led by a man named Hayes had been sent with the launch to look for water. After several weeks, the soldiers found an abundant supply of water. What they did not realize was that on the other island, Cornelisz, in an orgy of violence and bloodshed, had massacred 125 of the survivors who were not in sympathy with his plan. One man escaped and reached the third island to inform Hayes of what had happened. Cornelisz led two attacks on the island held by Hayes but was repelled. He then proposed a peace treaty, but during negotiations tried to corrupt the men faithful to Hayes. They warned their leader, and when Cornelisz arrived on the island to finalize the deal, his bodyguards were killed and the mutinous officer imprisoned.

Pelsaert returned, on board the *Sardam.* He

Irrefutable proof of the tragic end that befell the crew and passengers of the Batavia *has been gathered more on land than in the waters surrounding the wreck. On one of the islands of the Houtman Abrolhos, scientists discovered the remains of a young man who had been executed by sword. The story of this ship of the Dutch East Indies Company has become one of the most sensational in seafaring history.*

was about to go ashore in his service launch when Hayes managed to intercept and warn him. He barely had time to return aboard before Cornelisz's boats arrived. Once aboard the *Sardam*, Pelsaert fixed his guns on the mutineers. The men surrendered and were taken aboard and immediately put in irons. By September 18 they had all been arrested and all stolen jewels recovered. The mutineers were tried and executed on the island before the *Sardam* weighed anchor—except for two, who were marooned on the Australian continent.

The wreck of the *Batavia* was inspected and it was immediately clear that it was irretrievably lost: the keel and part of the upper works, dismantled by the waves, lay buried in a sand bank; the main mast had fallen across a rock in the opposite direction. Indian divers recovered eleven of the twelve chests of silver coins, leaving the last one—wedged in the coral—marked with an anchor and a cannon.

Australian interest in underwater archeology began in 1963 with the discovery of the *Batavia* and the *Vergulde Draeck*—a Dutch vessel shipwrecked in 1658 near the mouth of the Moore River in western Australia. The *Vergulde Draeck*'s treasure was recovered in a single season of excavation. The Australian government issued laws to protect the wrecks from raiders. The local museums became enriched with recovered items that confirmed the fact that the first explorations of the continent by Europeans dated back to more than one century before Captain Cook's voyages.

The *Batavia* was discovered in shallow waters north of Perth. Between 1973 and 1976, research and excavation efforts on the *Batavia* wreck were conducted by archeologists and the Western Australia Museum. The State Government built a base on Beacon Island—the same island that had previously been known as Batavia's Graveyard. An astonishing variety of ordnance, firearms, and projectiles was recovered during four campaigns conducted by archeologists. A section of the hull was found imbedded in the coral; navigational instruments and other items have made the wreck of the *Batavia* one of the most interesting finds in the history of marine archeology. In the Maritime Museum, a portal has been reconstructed, with two columns and a great triangular arch, out of sandstone blocks found on the wreck. In the end, one of the most fascinating features of the *Batavia* was that it served the double function of carrying commercial goods and being an armed vessel able to fight.

57

THE QUICKSILVER VESSELS

wo vessels set sail from the Spanish seaport of Cadiz in August of 1724, carrying mercury to be used in the process of refining gold and silver. They were the *Nuestra Señora de Guadalupe* and the *Conde de Tolosa*, and they were bound for Veracruz via Havana with a combined load of 400 tons of mercury, which would supply the mines for an entire year. On board the two vessels were 1,200 people between passengers and crew, supported by an arsenal of 144 cannon; the two vessels could sail with minimal risk in waters frequented by armed pirates attempting to seize Spanish property.

On the night of August 24, a hurricane hit the two vessels off Samaná Bay on the northeast coast of the Dominican Republic. Don Francisco Barrero y Pelaez, on board the *Guadalupe* as the official in charge of precious metals (including the mercury), thought that his time had come. What he did not realize was that the 250 tons of mercury on board would mean rescue for him and the ship. The oversized ballast filled with mercury caused the ship to float until it ran aground on a sandbar, sustaining little damage. Two days later, when the hurricane subsided, 550 out of the 650 people on board were safe and sound.

But the *Conde de Tolosa* suffered a different fate. The ship had anchored at the entrance to the bay, but the ropes of the anchors broke and the vessel was set adrift, its crew unable to steer it out of danger. The ship struck a great barrier reef that shattered the hull, killing most of the 600 people on board. The *Tolosa* sank, and the mainmast, undamaged, rose up straight out of the water. Eight men were able to climb to the top and remained there in the rigging for thirty-two days. When the rescue vessel arrived from Santo Domingo, seven had survived.

Tracy Bowden, an American diver, organized a research and recovery expedition for the two vessels some two and a half centuries later. In 1976 his company, Caribe Salvage, obtained the required permission of the government of the Dominican Republic to search for the wrecks. They assembled a team of divers, and began the expedition on board the *Hickory*.

They located the *Guadalupe* first. The mercury was blocked by a cargo of iron ship fittings, but the vessel yielded an amazing collection of eighteenth-century colonial artifacts. The team recovered coins, jewels, medals, lanterns, scissors, china, seals, guns, and some extremely delicate glassware. Bowden and his men worked on the wreck for an entire year. Then they began to think of the *Conde de Tolosa*.

In June of 1977 the magnetometer on board the *Hickory* surveyed the metallic mass of the *Tolosa*'s guns in the Samaná Bay. After three weeks' work, Bowden recovered a barrel the Spanish had filled with leather bags containing mercury. The *Tolosa*'s 150 tons of mercury would yield an estimated one million dollars. But Caribe Salvage found even greater treasure—1,000 pearls, diamond-studded brooches, a diamond-and-emerald pendant, and other gold jewelry. The Commission for Underwater Archaeological Recovery oversees the safe recovery of treasures from the waters of the Dominican Republic. The artifacts are now on display in the Casas Reales Museum in Santo Domingo.

For many, underwater treasure hunting is an entrepreneurial activity like any other. There is no shortage of sites to explore, thanks to the many Spanish galleons, loaded with riches, that sailed across the North Atlantic. When they encountered tropical hurricanes, the ships, often overloaded with cargo, were almost impossible to control in high winds and frequently would crash into the dangerous coral reefs around the islands. Those who are skilled at finding submerged treasure can always find investors to finance their expeditions—even, as with the Conde de Tolosa, *when the reward is a large load of mercury.*

The rich historical documentation gathered over the centuries about the trading that took place between Spain and the American colonies has allowed the accurate reconstruction of the routes followed by the Spanish galleons. Through this information, it has been possible to trace and often recover the precious cargo of the ships that sank in shallower waters. But even when the wreck lies deep, it can be easily accessible, like the Guadalupe and the Conde de Tolosa. Among the items recovered intact from the galleons were this engraved tumbler and wine decanter.

In the photographs on these and the following pages, divers work at recovering objects from the Conde de Tolosa *and the* Guadalupe. *On the right, two divers examine one of the large anchors, upon which is resting a terracotta amphora.*

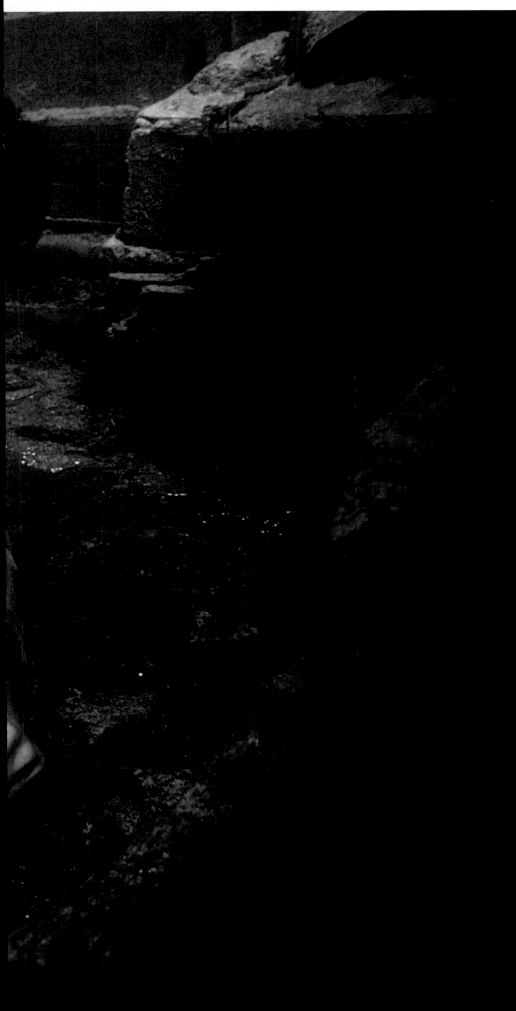

(Top left) *A pistol with brass side plates.* (Top right) *A gold doubloon.* (Left) *Tracy Bowden pours mercury in the depths at forty feet.* (Above) *A gold medallion, framed by twenty-four diamonds, bears the cross of the Order of Santiago. Diamond- and emerald-studded gold jewelry proved to be the greatest treasure of the galleons, although the primary cargo was mercury.*

The Hurricane that Killed the Forty-Niners

When, on September 12, 1857, the Central America *sank off the coast of South Carolina, America was becoming a strong new nation. Those who sought to find their fortunes in the gold rush in California would depart from New York and make the long journey by sea to Central America and on to the California mines. The* Central America *was a wooden ship that shuttled "forty-niners" between New York and Panama. The ship went down in a hurricane on a return trip to New York, with over a million dollars worth of gold coins and nuggets on board.*

Far away from the continental United States, 200 miles off the shores of South Carolina, at a depth of 8,500 feet, lies the wreck of the *Central America*. She was sunk by a hurricane in September of 1857. On board were 103 crew and 478 passengers. Of these, ninety-nine people were rescued before the ship sank. Another fifty-four were taken aboard by rescue ships. But 428 people—passengers and crew and Captain Lewis Herndon—died, many of them trying desperately to save their gold.

During the second half of the nineteenth century, adventurous emigrants from England, France, Italy, and Germany were traveling to America to make their fortunes, and the country was fast becoming a "melting pot." These were the years of the discovery of gold in the West, where millions of acres of land were available to anyone who was willing and able to cultivate them. The emigrants, some already American citizens and others soon to become so, lived mainly in the East, particularly in New York.

Midshipman Ruggiero Vitagliano Moccia, who embarked at the age of nineteen on a training cruise on board the Italian naval frigate *Urania*, described the city in his journal (published by Mursia in 1975): "The main city of the United States is New York, for its population, richness, size and trade . . . In 1790 it did not have more than 33,131 souls, in 1840 about 312,000 while nowadays (1845), its population has greatly increased. Forty thousand people work in its factories, as they are the principal source of income for its trade and oceanic navigations, in which 21,000 and 3,000 people are employed, respectively. It would be difficult to think of another American city as rich as this one, and if it is compared to the European capitals it can reasonably be at sixth place after London, Paris, Constantinople, Naples, and St. Petersburg for the number of its inhabitants."

New York was then basically what it is today—the heart of American business. At least a half million adventurous gold diggers (those who had money for passage) departed from New York harbor, going by sea to Central America, and from there to the Pacific coast and, eventually, the California mines. The Panama Canal had not yet opened. Once they found gold, they made the journey in reverse, exchanging their precious finds for dollars in New York.

In 1857, the *Central America* was one of two steam ships equipped with sails and paddle wheels that shuttled between New York and Panama. With an overall length of 272 feet, it was a wooden ship that weighed only 750 tons. It was innovative for those times—a luxury liner carrying the newly rich and their ladies, some of the legendary "forty-niners." Two months before its last journey, the ship had undergone numerous structural and cosmetic repairs in order to requalify it for international status.

On September 3 at four in the afternoon, the ship left Panama, spotlessly clean and bearing a new name. It moored at Havana on September 7 and the next morning departed for New York. Late in the day, a light wind started to blow from the west, and by nightfall it had become stronger. On the morning of September 9, the wind direction changed and powerful gusts caused the waves to break across the bow of the ship. By the next day, the passengers realized that the ship was in the middle of a dreadful storm. On September 11, the storm had become a full-fledged hurricane, and the sea took on the appearance of a watery mountain range.

The ship could not sail against the wind; it rolled helplessly in the hollows of the waves. The shutters of the hatches, their padlocks broken, opened and closed with the swaying of the hull. Ocean water began to pour in below decks. Soon the water was seeping into every opening on the ship, and by midday the bunkers at either end were flooded and the fuel was rendered unusable. Then the engines flooded, leaving the crew with no means of maneuvering the ship. Use of the sails was unthinkable. The crew and passengers went below and, side by side, bailed out the water from the cabins and the common rooms.

After dark, they began to launch signal rockets, hoping to capture the attention of a passing ship. On Saturday, September 12, the sky was partially cleared of heavy clouds, but the wind continued to blow with a growing fury. At midday, the captain admitted to a passenger—an ex-colleague of his in the armed forces—that the ship was lost. Soon after, the outline of a brig, the

Marine, appeared on the horizon.

Although the *Marine* had been seriously damaged by the hurricane, the captain was able to maneuver the ship toward the *Central America*. The crew lowered three of the ship's six lifeboats into the water, and the women, children, and a few other passengers were taken on board. The extraordinary skill and courage of the *Marine* crew brought these people to safety: on board lifeboats loaded with survivors, the men had to row for more than two hours against the forces of wind and current before they reached the *Marine*, saw the passengers safely on board, and pulled in the gangway behind them.

The two ships were soon set apart by the wind and the waves, and no other rescue attempt was possible. At eight o'clock that evening, the *Central America* listed twice, first to starboard, then to port. A huge wave washed over the ship. The bow was seen briefly, then the hull slipped under the surface forever.

In 1987, recovery of the treasure was undertaken by the Columbus-America Discovery Group, using an advanced sonar system to locate the wreck. The U.S. District Court granted the group the right to recover the gold.

THE *CARNATIC*

THE "SHUTTLE" FROM SUEZ TO BOMBAY

Today it might be called a shuttle-ship. In fact, this was exactly the task of the *Carnatic*: to meet, at Suez, the passengers and goods arriving in convoys by land from Port Said, (where they had landed after crossing the Mediterranean), and carrying them to India. There were just two months to go before the opening of the Suez Canal and the first performance of Giuseppe Verdi's *Aida*, composed to celebrate the opening of the direct passage between the Mediterranean and the Red Sea.

The *Carnatic* was typical of the ships built during the period of transition from sailing to steam-powered vessels. It was built in the Samuda Brothers shipyard in 1862 on behalf of the Peninsular & Oriental Steam Navigation Company. It was 291 feet long and thirty feet wide; it had a tonnage of 1,776 tons. It was equipped as a "hermaphrodite brig" (combining the characteristics of a brig and a schooner), with two bowsprits and a steam engine that delivered 1,870 horsepower, which moved a giant, three-bladed propeller, for a top speed of twelve knots.

The last voyage of the *Carnatic* lasted only a few hours. The ship sailed from Suez, headed towards Bombay, on Sunday, September 12, 1869, at ten in the evening with 230 passengers on board in addition to the crew. Just after noon the next day, Captain P. B. Jones was awakened by the exclamations of the duty officers: "Breakers at the bow, what should we do?" The captain ordered: "Helm to the left! Full speed astern!" The emergency maneuver lasted for only three minutes. They struck a coral reef, and the ship ran aground. The passengers were all on deck, but they remained calm. The crew decided to wait until daylight to try and free the ship. They worked for hours to lighten the prow. But the hull, because of the constant action of the tide, pressed down into the reef with more and more weight. The bilge slowly began to take on water.

In the meantime, life on board the ship went on as usual. Meals were served, and a passenger delegation asked the commander if they could all spend another night on board instead of disembarking for safe landing on a nearby island. They were expecting the *Sumatra*, another ship of the same shipping company, to come and rescue them. The captain agreed, but when, at two in

the morning, the water reached the steam boilers and extinguished them, he realized that the ship was lost. At daybreak the crew began transporting passengers to dry land.

But later that morning, disaster struck: the hull, weighed down by the water it had taken on, weakened by the incessant pounding of the waves, and no longer supported by the now-shattered reef, suddenly gave way and broke apart; the stern section rapidly sank to a depth of just over eighty feet. Twenty-seven people died. The survivors climbed onto the bow and waited their turn to be ferried to the island. On the island, cotton bales taken from the cargo were set on fire to attract the attention of the *Sumatra*, which had finally come into view. When all the survivors had left the scene, the other half of the *Carnatic* slid down to the seabed, reaching the stern, which had preceded it.

At that moment 40,000 pounds of gold sank among the Red Sea corals. Egyptian divers succeeded in recovering 32,000, but the rest is still hidden in unexplored areas. The gold is within reach of the many divers who explore the fascinating wreck and take from it the few remaining objects and instruments that have escaped the clutches of the coral.

The *Carnatic* was not positively identified until 1991, when it was visited by Andrea Ghisotti, an underwater photographer and journalist from Italy. After visiting the wreck for the first time, Ghisotti surfaced with a fragment of a plate, and through the trademark "Real Ironstone China" imprinted on the border, he began the process of research that would lead him to identify the ship.

The Carnatic *was a "hermaphrodite brig," having the combined characteristics of a brig and a schooner, that transported passengers between Suez and Bombay just prior to the opening of the Suez Canal. A hybrid that reflected the transition between sailing and steam-powered vessels, the ship resembled a clipper, but beneath its bow was a large, three-bladed propeller that is visible on the wreck today. The remainder of the wreck, whose planking has been partially destroyed by parasites, is now completely wrapped in a cloak of coral and other sea organisms.*

The Carnatic was a neglected wreck that went undiscovered for over a century; it still conceals some 8,000 pounds of gold. It was identified by Andrea Ghisotti, an Italian journalist and underwater photographer, in 1991. For its time, the Carnatic was a beautiful and modern ship, assigned to a special service that would terminate two months after its sinking with the opening of the Suez Canal. The ship ran aground in 1869; most of the passengers and crew were able to disembark before it actually sank on the following day.

DESTROYED BY
A VOLCANO

A splendid three-masted iron bark, the *Tamaya* was one of the last of its kind to sail the oceans with passengers and goods on board at a time when the great sailing ships had begun to disappear and be replaced with steam-powered ships. Today, the *Tamaya* lies 260 feet under the sea that washes over what used to be the roadstead of Saint-Pierre, capital of Martinique. The ship was destroyed on the morning of May 8, 1902—a morning as dark as the deep of night, when the sun was obscured by the smoke and ash of an erupting volcano—Mount Pelée.

Only thirty of the town's 30,000 inhabitants survived the disaster. Auguste Ciparis, a descendant of slaves, had been arrested and put into jail the previous night for being drunk and disorderly. He was dug out of the debris of his cell three days after the eruption, his body badly burned. He lived for many years to tell his story. Another survivor was a shoemaker named Léon Compère-Léandre. He dragged himself from the smoking ruins of his little shop and escaped to safety. Neither of the men actually saw the eruption as it was happening.

One eyewitness was Captain E. W. Freeman of the *Roddam*, which had arrived in Saint-Pierre early that morning. As his crew secured the *Roddam*, Freeman surveyed the other ships at anchor in the bay. They included the sailing ship *Gabrielle*, the Quebec Line *Roraima*, the *Tamaya*, and others. He remained on the bridge to enjoy the fresh air of the tropical morning, the warm sun and humidity mitigated by the trade winds. The bells of the cathedral tolled. It was Ascension Day. Captain Freeman looked at his watch. Two minutes to eight.

What he did not know was that the night before, after a violent quarrel with the French customs officer, who did not want to let him leave, Captain Antonio Ferrara, commander of the Italian ship *Orsolina*, had weighed anchor and sailed out to sea. Ferrara had grown up at the foot of Mount Vesuvius and knew about volcanoes. Mount Pelée had given him a bad feeling during the days he had spent in Saint-Pierre. When the customs officer had threatened to impose sanctions on him if he left the island without authorization, Ferrara had answered, "And who is going to impose them on me . . . you? Tomorrow you will all be dead!"

At a depth of 260 feet, the Tamaya *serves as a grim reminder of the appalling tragedy at Saint-Pierre in which nearly 30,000 people died. On the seabed near Saint-Pierre, just beyond the wreck of the* Tamaya, *are the wrecks of a dozen other ships destroyed in the disaster; they appear in the photographs on the following pages.*

Captain Freeman looked at the top of Mount Pelée and saw something he would never forget. The volcano erupted in a massive explosion that covered the entire city with burning volcanic ash within a matter of minutes. Of the fourteen ships at anchor in the bay, all but the *Roddam* were sunk or engulfed in flames. Freeman described the eruption as "a violent detonation that shook land and sea." The town was plunged into darkness.

Although the *Roddam* caught fire and several crewmen were killed or badly burned, Captain Freeman managed to maneuver his ship free of the harbor and head for Santa Lucía.

In the years since the devastating eruption, divers have explored the wrecks and have seen first-hand the effects of the intense fire from the explosion—melted glass, objects fused together, and charred wood. Among other objects, divers recovered the ship's bell from the *Tamaya*. Artifacts from this fascinating underwater graveyard will be displayed in the Vulcanological Museum in Saint-Pierre—a city that has rebuilt itself and today welcomes new ships into the bay where the *Tamaya* last dropped anchor.

THE SHIP THAT DISAPPEARED

**T**he disappearance of the *Yongala* was shrouded in mystery. Rumors that the ship had wrecked began on March 28, 1911, when the *Brisbane Courier*, a daily newspaper in Queensland, Australia, ran the headline: "NO NEWS OF THE *YONGALA*." The ship was last seen on the night of March 23, 1911, by the lighthouse keeper at Dent Island. It was on a northerly course, sailing from Melbourne to Cairns, had already made regular stops at Sydney, Brisbane, Mackay, and Bowen along the eastern coast, and it was scheduled to arrive in Townsville on March 24. During the evening of its disappearance, the entire area around the Whitsunday Islands was struck by a violent hurricane. Captain J. Sim, commander of the *Yongala*'s sister ship, the *Grantala*, had anchored in Bowling Green Bay. He would not learn of the disappearance of the *Yongala* until three days later, when he arrived in Brisbane.

A full-scale search began immediately. Police boats were sent to patrol the coastline, looking for signs of a wreck. The navy sent patrol boats and tugboats out into the ocean. No one could believe that the ship had vanished into thin air. Reassuring messages came from Sidney, where the shipping company that owned the *Yongala* was based: "You will see—the *Yongala* will be found again, safe and sound." It was believed that the commander, Captain William Knight, had steered the ship towards the open sea, beyond the Whitsunday Islands, but along the way, either because of engine failure or as a result of the hurricane, the ship had run aground on a coral reef.

By Tuesday, March 28, along the thirty-mile stretch of beach from Cape Bowling Green to Townsville, many items were found that were thought to have come from the missing ship. Surprisingly, some of the items had come from hold number three, the safest of all, proving that the keel of the ship had been split. Off shore, the tugboat *Alert*, which had sailed from Townsville, found kerosene cans, a life vest, two small wooden grates, two pillows with the mark A.S.S.Co. (Adelaide Steamship Company, the owner company), an oar, a barrel of oil, and a door with an engraved glass panel. The door was like those known to have been at the entrance to the music hall on board the ship. They were engraved with

The wreck of the Yongala *remains a mystery, as no reason for the ship's destruction has been established. In its resting place off Cape Bowling Green, the wreck appears remarkably intact except for its superstructures, which have been swept away by the currents. Today the* Yongala, *the most famous of the Australian wrecks, is a popular attraction for experienced divers and underwater photographers from all over the world.*

the Latin words *festina lente* and the date—1900. There was no doubt that the *Yongala* was lost forever, along with its 72 crew members and 48 passengers, its 686-ton cargo, and a purebred racehorse on its way to Townsville for the racing season. James Harvey, chairman of the Adelaide Steamship Company, told the company's shareholders that the loss of the *Yongala* was "one of the great unsolved sea mysteries."

On May 24, 1960, an official of the Australasian United Steam Navigation Co. wrote a letter to an acquaintance who worked for the Adelaide Steamship Company, in which he said: "I have recently been to Townsville, and I had the chance to learn, from one of the scuba divers diving on the *Yongala*, that the wreck lies at a depth of about 100 feet on a white sand floor, just off Cape Bowling Green. There are no coral cliffs nearby. The ship lies on its left side, with no apparent damage either to its right side or to the visible parts of its left side. An anchor is out of its eye and the helm is blocked. Someone who examined the wreck said that the ship may have capsized while trying to anchor. This opinion seems to disprove the theories that suggest the ship had badly hit the coral reef during the hurricane. When it met its terrible destiny, it certainly had nearly reached Townsville."

The wreck was declared of historic significance under the Historic Shipwrecks Act in June 1981. The *Yongala* has become one of the greatest attractions for diver-tourists from all over the world. The ship lies on a flat floor of white coral sand like an eerie, underwater lean-to: the left side acts as a roof, the upper deck, a wall. Sea organisms of every kind have attached themselves to the wreck. Thick clouds of bat fish follow divers from the surface down toward the seabed, where large schools of giant groupers, tangles of poisonous sea snakes, and restless sharks swim in and about the wreck. The sight is somewhat ominous—as if one were in the presence of a ghost ship.

THE UNSINKABLE SHIP ON HER MAIDEN VOYAGE

Dr. Robert D. Ballard, who first discovered the wreck of the *Titanic*, characterized it as "the great pyramid of the abyss." He was not only referring to the enormous size of the ship—882 feet long, 94 wide, and 100 high to the bridge level—but to the ship's tragic distinction as a grave site for the nearly 1,500 victims of the sinking on April 15, 1912.

The name *Titanic* is, for many, synonymous with the word "shipwreck." The wreck itself, although it is buried under two-and-a-half miles of water, has become a monument to human arrogance: the ship had a lifeboat capacity of 1,178—barely enough for half the number of passengers and crew on board during her maiden voyage—and the ship was considered by those who built it to be "absolutely unsinkable." Just before midnight on April 14, the ship struck an iceberg, and within less than an hour, began to sink. Shortly after 2:00 A.M., the ship broke in half; the bow section sank first, followed by the stern, and hundreds of lives were lost in what has been termed "the greatest maritime disaster in history."

Ballard's Franco-American team discovered and photographed the wreck on September 1, 1985. The first image was of a boiler; it was transmitted by a video camera on board the *Argo*, an underwater exploration device, and received on board the *Knorr*, an American oceanographic research ship carrying a science team from Woods Hole's Deep Submergence Laboratory. Co-leaders of the expedition were Ballard and Jean-Louis Michel. After the first image had been examined and the wreck positively identified, ANGUS (Acoustically Navigated Geological Underwater Survey) took extensive photographs of various details of the wreck and the debris field. Within a matter of hours, headlines announcing the discovery appeared in newspapers throughout the world.

The "*Titanic* Rush" began soon after the publication of the first photos taken by ANGUS. Families of the victims tried to organize exploratory expeditions. Enterprising profit-seekers dreamed up numerous schemes for raising the ship from her deep ocean grave. But the projected costs of these expeditions were prohibitive. Others had the idea of exploiting the wreck and transforming it into a tourist attraction—organized tours in bathyscaphes

The icy depths of the North Atlantic have transformed the once-magnificent Titanic *into a chilling ghost. Thought to be unsinkable, the ship went down during its maiden voyage on April 15, 1912, and has since become the most celebrated wreck in maritime history. Although popular theory holds that the ship struck an iceberg that inflicted irreparable damage to the starboard bow, many experts remain mystified as to how such a massive and "invincible" ship could have sunk so rapidly. The point of the bow is shown in the photograph on the right.*

As the ship was sinking, it broke in two; the bow section sank first and is deeply embedded in the sediments. The wreck lies in total darkness, two-and-a-half miles beneath the surface of the North Atlantic. The wreck of the Titanic was discovered on September 1, 1985 by a Franco-American team led by Robert Ballard and Jean-Louis Michel.

In the photograph on the right is the open window of a first-class cabin, the glass still intact. Shown below is the enormous port bow anchor draped in long, fingerlike rusticles.

that could accomodate several passengers—the cost of the fare, a mere $25,000.

In 1986, Ballard returned to the wreck to continue the work he had already begun. He explored the wreck site on board the *Alvin*, a manned submersible, using a robot connected to the submersible by means of a tether. The robot enabled the three-man crew of the *Alvin* to control a camera and a mechanical arm that could pick up even very small objects.

Subsequent expeditions by other teams have enabled scientists to speculate about the manner in which the ship actually sank. Because of the thousands of tons of water that poured in through the hole made by the iceberg, the *Titanic* broke in half. The bow section reached the ocean floor first, plowing into the mud. The stern section, after rising up as if to touch the night sky, slid quietly into the sea.

But examination of the wreck has prompted other theories as well. The torn plates of the hull appear to be turned outward, as if destroyed by a blast (the icy water coming into contact with the overheated boilers may have caused such a blast). In fact, the iceberg should have caused the plates to implode, pushing the edges inward. Scientists continue to examine pieces of the wreck in an attempt to discover how the "unsinkable" ship could have been destroyed with such seeming ease.

Scientific expeditions to the wreck site have provided new opportunities for the development and use of sophisticated underwater lighting, photographic, filming, and deep-diving recovery equipment. In 1987, Robert Chappaz, owner of Taurus Internationale, a small company in Paris that installs off-shore oil rigs, and his partner, Yves Corner, organized an expedition supported by IFREMER, the French National Institute of Oceanography. The most difficult part of the project was securing funds to cover the costs. Chappaz found the right man in Greenwich, Connecticut—George Tulloch, a passionate Francophile, who assembled a group of investors and raised the necessary six million dollars. IFREMER placed its extraordinary technical instruments at the disposal of the team—on board the *Nautile* bathyscaphe equipped with "Robin," a small robot able to take photographs and record videotapes.

Planning for the *Nautile* dates back to 1978; it was built at a cost of seventeen million dollars. The submersible was first put into service in 1985. It has a thirteen-hour operation capacity per dive, a fifteen-mile range, and can travel at a speed of twenty-five knots. It can accommodate three crew members. Perhaps its most valuable asset is the efficiency of its mechanical arms. But during the 1987 expedition, the arms were only used to salvage small objects (a total of 900) from the wreck and the debris field. This was in honor of Ballard's wishes; in 1987, two years after discovering the wreck, he testified before the United States Congress in support of legislation that proclaimed the *Titanic* an international memorial. Ballard maintained that the scattered objects on the ocean floor must be salvaged and recorded without being damaged. He added: "No attempt must be permitted to bring the ship back to the surface or to look for and salvage the objects inside it. The wreck is no more the beautiful lady that sailed on her maiden voyage. It is no longer a four-day-old ship. It lost its beauty but not its majesty. Let it lie where it is lying, without being touched again, ever."

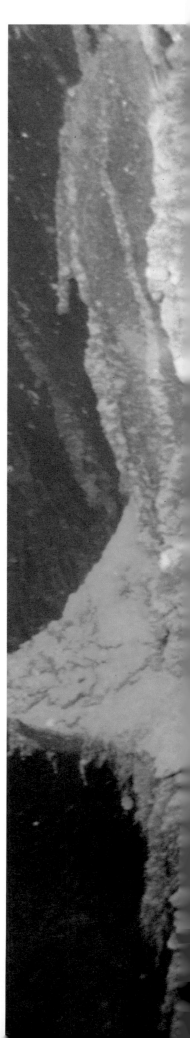

The photograph below reveals the descent-damaged railing along the bow of the ship. This sequence of images was taken by the remote-controlled vehicle ANGUS. The top photograph on the right shows two of the Titanic's large cranes, which were used to load and off-load cargo from the ship.

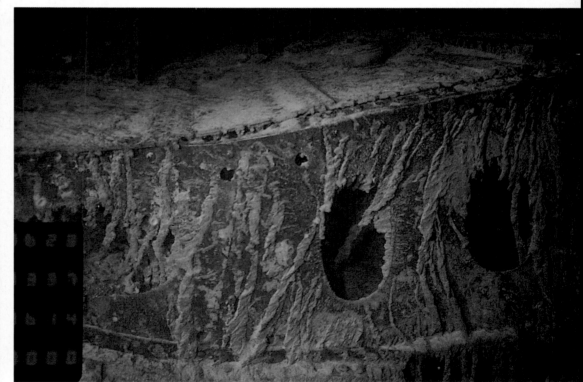

WORLD WAR I PRIVATEER

Privateers should not be confused with pirate ships. Privateers were employed during the conduct of war; they were private ships authorized by a government to attack and capture enemy vessels. Perhaps the last great privateer was the well-known "pocket battleship," the *Admiral Graf von Spee*, sunk at the mouth of the Rio de la Plata in 1939. The Germans had perfected this way of fighting through private ships. A forerunner of the *Graf von Spee*, a small cruiser, was the *Emden*. After the Franco-Prussian war in 1870, Germany had succeeded in assembling an empire; in order to protect its territories, the government employed the Imperial Cruiser Squadron; it was based in Tsingtao, a Chinese port, to which the *Emden* was sent in 1910.

The beginning of World War I caught the German forces stationed in the Far East by surprise. The admiral and commander of the Squadron directed the entire fleet toward South America, but ordered Commander Karl von Müller, Captain of the *Emden*, to go to the Indian Ocean with the aim of destroying enemy ships—in short, for privateering. First, the *Emden* had to stock up on coal, which it did on September 6, 1914, by seizing the Greek steamer *Pontoporos*, which was carrying 6,000 tons of coal to Calcutta.

During the following three days, the *Emden* sank five British steamers. The Allies decided to outfit a naval squadron to put an end to the *Emden*'s raids: it was composed of three British armored cruisers, an armored cruiser from France, and a Japanese battle cruiser. But the *Emden* was elusive. On September 22 it sank a tanker from Madras and then threw the British cargo boats in the Bengala Gulf into confusion. Then, with extraordinary boldness, it presented itself in a port of one of Chagos Islands, a British archipelago, to take on fresh water and food, taking advantage of the fact that the residents of the island had not yet learned of the war. Later, the *Emden* sailed to the Fiji Islands and sank the Russian cruiser *Scmetsciung* and the French fighter *Mousquet*. In London, an angry Admiral Jerran decided to gather a formidable naval force to defeat the *Emden*.

Meanwhile, the commander of the *Emden* steered his cruiser toward Direction Island in the Cocos (Keeling) Islands, northwest of Australia, to

The *Emden* was a small cruiser employed by the Germans during World War I as a privateer vessel—a private ship that sought out and destroyed enemy ships. It earned quite a reputation as a warship and did a great deal of damage before it was fired upon, in November of 1914, by the Australian cruiser Sydney.

The *Emden* fired the first shot, crippling the Australian ship and, remarkably, the captain of the *Emden* stopped to rescue the Sydney's crew while steering his wounded ship to land. As the *Emden*'s career as a warship ended, its captain was praised for his extraordinary behavior in the face of defeat.

destroy the radio and telegraph station there.

The *Emden* had just begun to bombard the target when the Australian cruiser *Sydney* came into view on the horizon. The *Emden* turned its cannon against the enemy ship and struck a decisive blow. But the commander of the *Sydney* was confident that his larger and more powerful warship would prevail. He immediately returned fire. The *Emden* was mortally wounded: the deck was shattered; two of the three funnels collapsed; the mainmast and the stern observation post fell to one side of the ship; and the forebridge was demolished. The commander, realizing that all was lost, decided to steer his broken ship to the North Keeling Reef so that the crew could disembark. But first he collected the crew of the *Sydney*, which had been disabled by the *Emden*'s initial fire.

On November 9, 1914, the *Emden*'s career as warship ended forever. Among the crew, 136 men were killed, 65 were wounded, and 117 surrendered to the Australians. The wreck, now considered a monument, lies on the reef off North Keeling Island. One side lies submerged as a result of the breakers; that side lies at a depth of thirty feet from the ocean's surface, the cannons pointed toward the open sea.

In Australia today, a positive feeling about the German ship and its epic deeds still remains. Each year on November 9, those in the "*Emden* family" gather; they are the descendents of the soldiers on both sides. In 1921 in Germany, the survivors of the *Emden* were allowed to add the ship's name to their surname, as if it were a title of nobility.

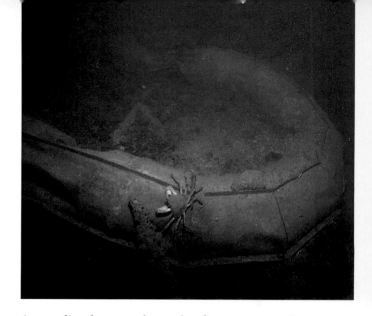

THE *ROYAL OAK*

A SURPRISE ATTACK AT SCAPA FLOW

Scapa Flow is a small expanse of sea within the Orkney Islands. Across the Pentland Firth is the northern coast of Scotland. Scapa Flow is an ideal natural harbor for sheltering a fleet, and in modern times, it has been designated for this purpose by the Royal Navy of Scotland. After the defeat of the Central Empires—Germany and Austria—in the First World War, the German warships anchored at Scapa Flow were sunk on June 17, 1919, by order of Admiral Reuter, who could not bear the humiliation of defeat. The English tried to recover some of them, at least those in the most shallow water. A number of small family concerns were established in the Orkney Islands with the aim of recovering the scrap metal from the German vessels. But none of them realized any significant profit from the venture; they went out of business, and the Kaiser's ships were left alone.

With the outbreak of the Second World War, the Orkney Islands and Scapa Flow remained key to the strategy of the Royal Navy: the narrow passages between the islands were considered impenetrable by armed ships and submarines because they were so heavily guarded; the only threat came from the skies above—the enemy air force. But the most unexpected and bold attack came from the sea—more specifically, from under water.

On the night of October 14, 1939, thirty-year-old lieutenant Günther Prien, commander of a German U-boat—a submarine—entered Scapa Flow through the canal at Kirk Sound, using the tide and the dark of night to his advantage. His target was a British battleship—the *Royal Oak*. A floating fortress, the ship was equipped with two turrets—one at the bow and one at the stern, each with four fifteen-inch cannon—and antiaircraft guns. It carried a crew of 1,000 men and could cut through the sea at a speed of twenty knots.

Construction of the *Royal Oak* was begun on January 15, 1914, in the naval dockyards at Devonport, near Plymouth; the ship was launched on November 17, 1915. After the First World War it was modernized and, following a training exercise in the North Sea, was sent to Scapa Flow to provide antiaircraft cover for other ships.

When Commander Prien looked through his periscope and saw the outline of the *Royal Oak* in the moonlight on the water of Scapa Flow, he immediately gave the order for two torpedoes to be launched at the target. It was one o'clock in the morning. The torpedoes struck the outer armor of the ship but did not cause significant damage. The crew of the *Royal Oak*, not suspecting that they were under fire, thought that there had been two explosions on board, and confusion reigned on board the ship. The Germans took advantage of the delay caused by the chaos and launched a second round of torpedoes that ripped into the *Royal Oak*, causing irreparable damage.

The ship began to list, taking on enormous amounts of water below the waterline, and then to sink, from the combined weight of the water and her powerful cannon. It was swallowed by the sea within minutes. Since that night, it has been lying on its side, ninety-eight feet down, its superstructures destroyed, its hull clearly visible under only sixteen feet of water. For some months after the sinking, the ship was surrounded by nets set out to capture the bodies of the crew as they surfaced.

Commander Prien's return to his German port was broadcast live on German radio: "At this moment we are witnessing the submarine crew's salute. To the sound of 'Deutschland Über Alles' this excellent ship is coming into port—the U-boat that, a few days ago, caught the world by surprise and sank the British battleship *Royal Oak*. The Commander-in-Chief of the Navy—Admiral Räder—stands at the head of the line of officials saluting the ship passing in front of us."

After over fifty years, the slow release of diesel fuel from the wreck continues. Today the *Royal Oak* is a war memorial for the Royal Navy.

Scapa Flow is remembered for its role in the Second World War, not because it was the site of a great battle, but because it was the site of a surprise attack that resulted in the sinking of the Royal Oak, *a British battleship. The operation, led by Captain Günther Prien, was the result of many years of patient work. Captain Alfred Wehring, who spent five years posing as a clockmaker in a village in the Orkney Islands, supplied the Germans with the necessary information to successfully carry out the mission.*

The ice-cold waters of Scapa Flow, a known haven for the ships of the Royal Navy, is now also a silent graveyard for ships and seamen, a sad commentary on the consequences of war. In these shallow waters are the wrecks of several ships of the defeated German Imperial Navy—scuttled in 1919 to avoid the humiliation of surrender. Among them lies the wreck of the Royal Oak, sunk at the beginning of the Second World War; it went down with its crew on October 13, 1939. Later in the war, the German U-boat that sank the Royal Oak suffered an equally tragic fate; after being fired upon by a British destroyer, it never surfaced again.

THE *UMBRIA*

Scuttled in the Face of War

"I was suspended over the blue-black abyss. Beneath me, one side of the ship was facing upward; the other side had disappeared in the darkness of the seabed. A very large funnel pointed diagonally toward the surface and was entangled in coral. Even deep in the inner part of the funnel the marvelous corals had grown, developing in large quantities and in great variety. Thousands of small fish swam among the coral structures. I was in a hurry. I went straight toward the deck. At a depth of sixty-five feet, I felt as light as a bird, and I sat on the foghorn of the ship for a few minutes because I was impressed by such magnificence. It was a huge ship lying in the bosom of the sea covered by corals. I could imagine how it would be in fifty or a hundred years. The corals would continue to grow, closing the openings in the plates. In 200 years, the ship would be nothing but a strange coral rock."

Hans Hass, the great Austrian pioneer of underwater diving and a writer, photographer, and cinematographer, described his impressions of the *Umbria* in this way. It was 1949, and the ship had been lying in the Red Sea off Port Sudan since June 10, 1940, when its commander, Captain Lorenzo Muiesan from Trieste, had heard Mussolini's voice on the radio announcing the declaration of war.

The *Umbria* had sailed from Naples on May 28 in the evening, carrying armored vehicles, provisions, and equipment for the Italian troops stationed in east Africa. The ship carried weapons as well: there were 300,000 bombs and 60 cases of incendiary devices. Included in the supplies were some twenty boxes of the currency Italy had adopted for use in the east African colonies; it would be used to pay the soldiers stationed in the port of Massaua.

At the entrance to the Suez Canal, the British, who controlled the region, had required a check on the cargo of the *Umbria*; they knew that Italy was going to war, together with the Third Reich, against them. Captain Muiesan was compelled to welcome the Royal Navy inspector on board. That first inspection was superficial, and the *Umbria* was allowed to pass. But it was escorted by the armed sloop *Grimsby*.

On June 9, 1940, in the late afternoon, the

The Umbria *is "the perfect wreck"—an excellent training ship for divers and underwater photographers. It sank without violence—without being mortally wounded by torpedoes or bombs, without striking a reef. The ship was scuttled on the order of its captain, who did not want it to fall into enemy hands. In its location near Port Sudan in the Red Sea, the wreck is easily recognizable and accessible, as it lies very near the surface. Even novice divers can enter the main deck and the outer cabins of the wreck. Exploration of the inner rooms and the holds is more complicated but also more fascinating.*

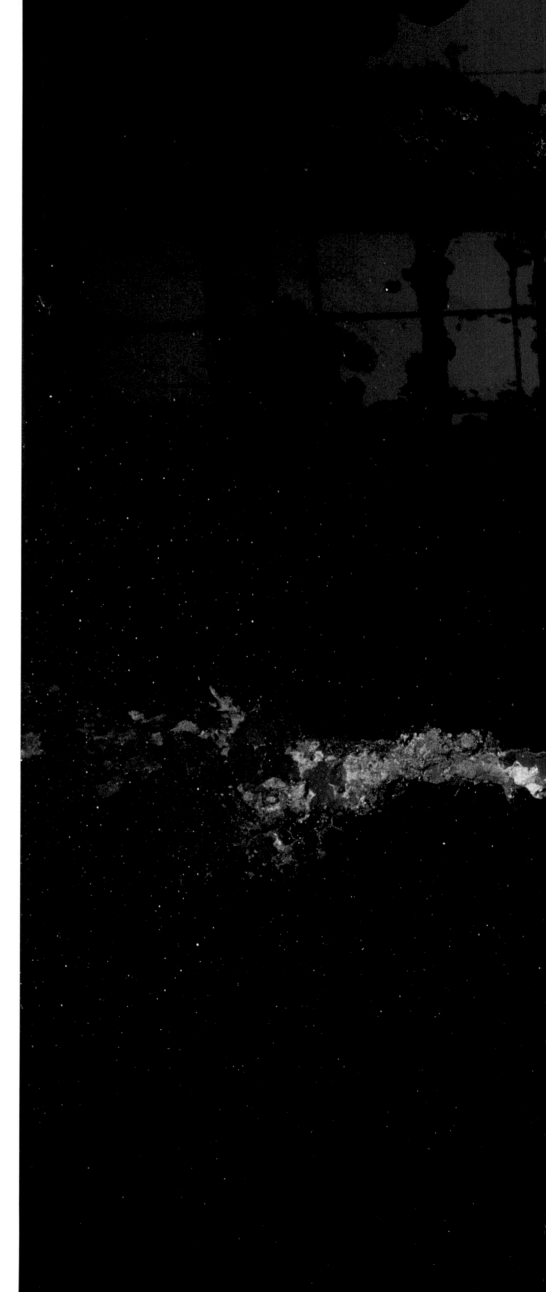

*Many fish have become perma-
nent inhabitants of the wreck.
They have become so accustomed
to the presence of divers that they
pester visitors for food and pose
obligingly for photographs.*

Italian ship was stopped again, near Port Sudan,
this time by the *Leander*. Boarding the ship was
Lieutenant Stevens, followed by a group of twen-
ty-two armed soldiers. Their intentions were
clear: they planned to take possession of the ship
as soon as hostilities broke out. Captain Muiesan
was carrying no passengers, and he found accom-
modations on board for those who at any moment
might become his enemies.

   On the following night, Captain Muiesan
heard the news in a radio broadcast from Rome.
He had only a few hours to arrange the destruction of his ship; he knew he could not take any
other action. After ordering the crew to burn the
ship's documents, he ordered the first mate and
the chief engineer to sink the ship. He then went
to Lieutenant Stevens and urged him to order a
rescue drill. While all the men, both English and
Italian, were on deck for the drill and waiting to
be lowered in the lifeboats, a British soldier
appeared and excitedly informed the lieutenant
that the ship was taking on water. The drill
became a rescue operation.

   Once in the lifeboat headed for the *Grimsby*,
Muiesan told the truth to Stevens, who had not
heard the news: "Our two countries are at war."
Muiesan would be a prisoner of war until 1945,
when he returned to his native Trieste.

   The *Umbria* was neither big nor beautiful—
even if its first underwater explorer, Hans Hass,
thought it was. It was a steam-powered cargo ship
built at the end of the nineteenth century, and
bore the awkward lines typical of the cargo ships
from that period.

   After the commander destroyed the ship, the
Umbria became one of the most beautiful wrecks
in the world. The wreck has changed since 1949
when Hans Hass visited it. Tourists who are divers
can witness these transformations, as they move
carefully with their cameras into the ship's holds
and swim weightless among the superstructures.
Ships lying in the waters of the Red Sea are covered over by corals and other sea organisms, but
they are also renewed by this random, vigorous,
and almost fanciful growth.

A picture of Italy as a country at war in the forties is still frozen into the objects lying within the wreck of the Umbria. In its holds, together with a cargo of bombs (shown at right), the ship still harbors three automobiles—one can be seen in the top left photograph below. Pictured below the car is a section of the galley.

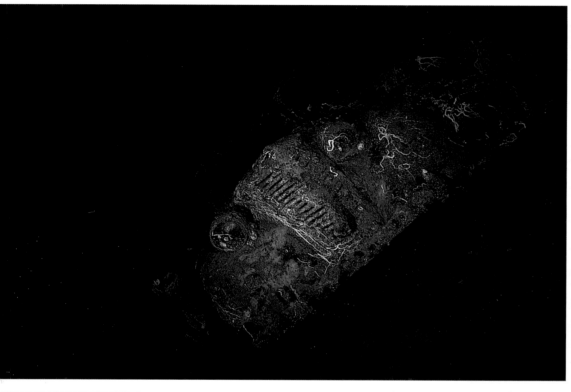

DEADLY MINES
AT ESPIRITU SANTO

The President Coolidge *hastily changed roles in 1942 from a passenger ship for Americans who wanted to visit the Far East to a troop carrier in the Second World War. On its way to deliver troops and weapons to Guadalcanal, the ship struck two mines in the port of Espiritu Santo. The beautiful, manmade details of the elegant ship* President Coolidge *are now part of the tropical underwater environment. Deprived of its wooden frame (shown on this page in a photo from the ship's advertising brochure) by teredo worms, the delicate Elizabethan figure over the fireplace in the main hall of the ship now smiles upon the divers who visit the wreck.*

he *President Coolidge* was an elegant American passenger ship that sailed from San Francisco to the Far East. It was pressed into service during the Second World War as a troop carrier, and in preparation for this new role, was stripped of many of its beautiful appointments, including rich wood paneling, silk draperies, and cut-glass fixtures. The ship sailed across the Pacific in fourteen days, and entered the port of Espiritu Santo (an island in what is now Vanuatu) on October 26, 1942.

It was a bright, tropical morning. The ship was carrying weapons and equipment for the troops at Guadalcanal, but its primary "cargo" consisted of 5,440 soldiers. At 9:30 sharp it entered the seaport—a base of vital importance for the Allied forces. Suddenly, from his position on the bow, First Lt. Web Thompson saw a blinker light flashing on the shore, but the code was too fast for him to read.

The desperate signal being sent from the shore—"You have just entered a mine field"—could not be repeated before the *President Coolidge* struck two mines in rapid succession. One of the firemen on board, Robert Reid, was killed in the explosion. The lights went out, the engines stopped, and communications channels were interrupted. Just under two hours later, the ship slowly began to sink at the stern and find its way down to the channel floor. The captain went down with the ship and was posthumously awarded the Distinguished Service Cross.

The cargo, including gas masks, submachine and machine guns, antiaircraft guns, magazines, cartridges, bombs, and helmets, is still on the wreck—blocking the promenade deck, filling the holds, the cabins, and the halls, at a depth of 147 feet. These weapons and trappings of war, and what was once a beautiful passenger ship, are now a part of the tropical environment of the Pacific.

Assigned to carry troops and weapons to supply the Allied forces engaged in the Pacific, the President Coolidge *was equipped with defensive weapons such as this three-inch antiaircraft gun.*

A diver lifts and illuminates one of several steel helmets found on the promenade deck. The inner chambers of the once-beautiful ship are encrusted with sea life and covered with a brown-green dust. *(Overleaf) The deck of the* President Coolidge, *with empty lifeboat davits reaching out into the sea like giant tentacles.*

THE STARS AND STRIPES VS. THE RISING SUN

he Second World War was truly a global war for the United States—more so than for any other country involved in the conflict. The Americans fought from Africa to Europe, but the most important military theater for the U.S. in that war was the Pacific Ocean. It borders the country's entire west coast, and includes, in addition to Hawaii, the Philippines, Guam, the Caroline Islands, the Marianas, New Guinea, the Solomon Islands, and the Bismarck Archipelago—the entire constellation of islands under Allied influence. It was in the Pacific that the Americans suffered the devastating attack on Pearl Harbor by Japan.

Therefore, it was in the Pacific that the "stars and stripes" pitted all of its military power against

In the photograph below, a diver investigates an American Bell P-39 shot down during an attack on the Japanese fleet at anchor in Hansa Bay, Papua New Guinea. Pictured on the right is the wreck of an American bomber lying in

the shallow waters near Saipan Island in the Pacific. On the following page, in the waters of the Bismarck Sea near New Guinea, an American B-17 bomber appears to have sustained damage only in the nose section. This aircraft is said to have been shot down during the attack on the Japanese fortress at Rabaul. The entire crew survived.

the "rising sun." And, lying on the floor of that ocean, is the tragic evidence of the violence of the war—hundreds of ships and planes that were lost on either side, sunk or shot down by the enemy.

Early in 1942, Japanese forces took possession of Rabaul on New Britain Island, taking thousands of prisoners and seizing both air and naval bases. From there they launched an attack on Port Moresby, but they were repelled in a four-day air conflict known as the Battle of the Coral Sea.

The Japanese seized Guadalcanal in July; American marines landed on the island in August.

The fighting was bitter, and control of the island went back and forth for several months, but by February 1943, the United States had cleared Guadalcanal of Japanese troops. Many planes and ships were lost during those weeks; for this reason, the canal in which forty-eight lost ships and aircraft have been located was nicknamed "Ironbottom Sound."

In the Battle of the Bismarck Sea, fought in March, 1943, Japanese soldiers tried to reach New Guinea from Rabaul, but Allied forces inflicted heavy losses to their convoys and then built a ring of bases around Rabaul, rendering it powerless. But the Americans paid dearly for their success; they suffered significant losses of men and equipment in the battles fought in the Pacific, which were almost always decided by the offensive potential of the aircraft carriers that launched the fighters from their decks against the enemy.

Since the end of the war, corals have seized upon the battleships, aircraft carriers, submarines, fighter bombers, and combat planes that are scattered throughout the Pacific, making them into fixed abodes. On the floor of the world's largest and deepest ocean lie the wrecks of hundreds of ships and planes that fought in the Pacific theater. Perhaps some of them will be discovered by chance—by divers or manned submersibles on scientific missions. Then we will be able to see their images, as we do here, fixed in photographs, or on film—reminders of the enormous toll taken by the most devastating war in history.

In the Second World War the expanse of sea between New Guinea and the Solomon Islands was the scene of vigorous fighting between American and Japanese forces. In January 1942, a Japanese contingent took possession of Rabaul on the island of New Britain, setting up a garrison of 100,000 men, five airports, and one naval base. From here the Japanese tried to invade the Allied base at Port Moresby, New Guinea, but they were repelled in the Battle of the Coral Sea. In March 1943, at the end of the battle of the Bismarck Sea, the Allies bombed Rabaul. Today the seabed of Rabaul is a vast tangle of ravaged wrecks. These photographs are of the Hakki Maru, a Japanese vessel bombed by a B-25 on January 17, 1944.

THE LAGOON OF THE SETTING SUN

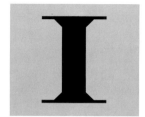

In a coral lagoon in the Truk Islands in the western Pacific Ocean, just above the equator, lies a fleet of sixty Japanese ships that were sunk in 1944. The site is known by scuba divers around the world as Truk Lagoon and constitutes the world's largest collection of artificial reefs. Although it is a paradise for diving enthusiasts, it is at the same time a monument to the memory of the thousands of Japanese sailors who died during the attack that was known as "Operation Hailstone."

The huge masses of rusty iron in the clear, calm waters of Truk Lagoon are the tragic remains of the United Fleet of the Japanese Imperial Navy. This lagoon, enclosed by a ring of coral and surrounded by a luxuriant tropical jungle, is the graveyard of many still-unidentified vessels, including cargo ships, cruisers, destroyers, and armored tankers.

From 1942 until the attack by the American Navy and Air Force, the Japanese had stationed their primary fleets in this location. The fleet was comprised of aircraft carriers, battleships, heavy cruisers, and several logistical ships charged with the refueling and maintenance of this extraordinary armed force. The United States military clearly understood the importance of Truk from a strategic standpoint. If those ships had been allowed to remain there, the Japanese could not only successfully support their land forces engaged in driving back the assaults of General McArthur, but also lead destructive operations in other areas of the Pacific.

In Washington, two plans circulated among the military strategists: the first advocated the taking of Truk Island and using it as an American base; the second would involve the neutralization of the Japanese naval force by attacking it through an extraordinary deployment of forces. The Americans regarded Truk as the "Gibraltar of the Pacific"—an impenetrable base—so the second plan prevailed. At the same time, the Japanese were aware that their fortifications could not sustain a grand-scale air-sea attack.

On February 4, 1944, a U.S. Marine scout bomber carried out a photographic survey of the lagoon. The images revealed to the Americans the presence of a battleship, two aircraft carriers, five or six heavy cruisers, four light cruisers, twenty

The waters of Truk Lagoon protect an extraordinary military museum of the Second World War, accessible to anyone able to dive with an aqualung. Some of the wrecks, both ships and airplanes, are so close to the surface they can be observed from the safety of a glass-bottom boat. Shown here is the three-inch bow gun of the San Francisco Maru.

torpedo-boat destroyers, twelve submarines, and a large number of support ships—all at anchor in the lagoon. The reconnaissance flight did not go unnoticed; Admiral Mineichi Coga, commander of the United Fleet, realized that an American attack was imminent. On February 10, he ordered most of his battleships to Palau, and he left for Japan on board the *Musashi*, sister ship of the famous *Yamato*.

Operation Hailstone began soon after daybreak on February 17, 1944. The American and English

down. Others were blocked on the runways. The runways of other islands of Truk were bombarded with such intensity that only 100 of the 365 airplanes on the ground were left undamaged. A second wave of fighters inflicted such extensive damage that it was afterwards impossible for the planes that had escaped destruction to use the airfields. And immediately after the second, a third wave of fighters, bombers, and torpedo-bombers descended on the lagoon.

After the third wave, the rest of that day was quiet. But in the early morning hours of the following day, bombers took off from the decks of the American aircraft carriers; it was the first night attack in the history of these ships. Its effects were devastating, causing more than thirty percent of the total damage inflicted on the fleet. The cargo boat *Aikoku Maru* sank immediately; a bomb had hit the magazine. The explosion was so violent that it destroyed the plane that had released the bomb. The cargo boat *Kiyosumi Maru* was turned on its side from a hit beneath its waterline. Bombs or torpedoes sank the *Heian Maru* and the *Rio de Janeiro Maru*, both submarine support ships. The aircraft carrier *Fujikawa Maru*, at anchor for repairs, began to sink within a few minutes, its right side destroyed by a torpedo.

A series of bombings of land targets by daylight completed Operation Hailstone. The Americans had sunk 200,000 tons of ships, rendered the island uninhabitable, and prevented the Japanese from launching a counterattack.

Today Truk Lagoon is an underwater museum that can be visited by divers, who can first review a list of the names of ships within safe diving range. Divers can see and even touch the ships, but they must explore the wrecks with caution (some of the ships still carry explosives) and with respect, taking care to replace any object picked up and examined during the dive. The lagoon has been designated a historical monument; artifacts on the wrecks are protected by law.

aircraft carriers *Bunker Hill*, *Enterprise*, *Yorktown*, *Essex*, and *Intrepid*, under the command of Vice-Admiral R. A. Spruance and Rear Admiral M. A. Mitscher, stood waiting ninety miles northwest of Dublon Island, the most important Japanese operational station at Truk. Sixty-two Hellcat torpedo-boat destroyers were launched against the fleet at anchor in the lagoon. The first air raid had to destroy the Japanese aircraft on the ground and then take control of the air space over the lagoon.

During the first attack, the more than thirty Japanese planes that were able to take off were shot

Before diving in the lagoon, one can look at the catalogue that contains the names of the major ships within reach of divers with aqualungs. They include the Fujikawa Maru, *the* Yamagiri Maru, *the* San Francisco Maru, *the* Sankisan Maru, *the* Rio de Janeiro Maru, *the* Shinkoku Maru, *the* Amagisan Maru, *the* Hanakawa Maru, *the* Gosei Maru, *the* Seiko Maru, *and the* Aikoku Maru.

CALVI, CORSICA

WHERE THE FLYING FORTRESS ENTERED THE SEA

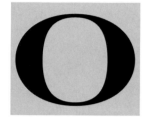

O n November 24, 1943, a squadron of 105 B-17s was flying toward the coast of France. They took off from the Allied base at Foggia, in southern Italy, and headed toward their assigned target—a German submarine base at Toulon. The planes, known as "Flying Fortresses," were filled to capacity with bombs. That night, German Messerschmitts intercepted the American planes. The ensuing air battle was one of many fought during the Second World War.

One of the Flying Fortresses, hit by enemy fire and losing altitude, sent a radio message to the control tower at the airport at Calvi, in Corsica, asking them to prepare for an emergency landing. But the only working engine could not sustain the aircraft any longer, and the plane began to plummet toward the open sea. The captain had no alternative but to try and land on the water. He released the bombs as the plane was about to make contact with the sea. The impact of the landing severed the tail from the plane. Seven out of the nine crewmen aboard dove into the water and survived. The plane became one of many from the Second World War to be "buried" at sea.

Twenty years later, in the summer of 1963, Paul Valeani, a scuba diver from Corsica, found the wreck of the Flying Fortress, lying nearly intact on the ocean floor. Inside, he found the remains of the two dead soldiers, still dressed in their flight suits. When the news of the discovery reached an American base in Germany, Paul Valeani was asked to recover the bodies for proper burial.

In the waters off Marseille lies the wreck of a badly damaged German Messerschmitt—perhaps the same one that shot down the Flying Fortress.

A number of the aircraft shot down during the Second World War are in the Mediterranean, mainly along the French coast. One such plane—a Boeing B-17 Flying Fortress (pictured at right)—rests at the bottom of the sea near Calvi, in southern Corsica. The U.S. Air Force flew these powerful four-engine bombers in massive numbers. Toward the end of the conflict, in the spring of 1945, the much more lethal B-29s were already in operation. On the following page is the wreck of a Messerschmitt BF-109, a German fighter considered to be the enemy par excellence *of the Flying Fortress.*

The Sinking of the "*K.T.*"

Giuseppe Chiappare ("Napoli" to his friends), a fisherman from Sestri Levante, saw the ship go down. He recalls that it was a cold morning in April 1944, at seven o'clock. The ship, perhaps a small French minesweeper that had been captured by the Germans, seemed to be headed for the village, escorted by two antisubmarine motorboats. The escorts were not keeping careful watch, however, because an Allied submarine appeared suddenly and launched two torpedoes against the ship they were guarding. The sea where Chiappare was trying to earn his living suddenly became a war zone: one torpedo hit the small ship aft, and the other struck the coastline, turning the water silver with dead fish.

Chiappare remembers that the ship, called the *K.T.* (no one knows the ship's true name; the letters *K.T.* were engraved on objects found on the wreck), sank very fast, but without loss of life; the crew was picked up by the two escort boats.

In the intervening years, the *K.T.* has been stripped of much of its cargo and furnishings. The wreck lies at a depth of 183 feet and so is accessible only to skilled and experienced divers. The delicate, tapered bow maintains its fragile beauty, and the ship's antiaircraft guns are adorned with bright yellow sea anemones. Along the hull, other light cannon and machine guns are home to colonies of sea anemones—a brilliant flowering garden that seems to pay tribute to the anonymous ship. The stern, which sustained most of the damage from the torpedo, is less accessible in that it has settled deep into the seabed. Exploration of the internal part of the ship is a dangerous undertaking. Through a narrow passageway is the engine room, where everything is still in its place—the radio through which the captain transmitted orders from the bridge, the controls and gauges—exactly as they were at the moment of impact.

A second wreck lies in the waters off Sestri Levante. It is a cargo boat that, like many others, undoubtedly carried troops during the war. In November 1943, it was attacked and sunk by a squadron of Allied planes and ended up on the muddy seabed at a depth of 118 feet. Only the bow remains.

The wreck of a modern warship always has special appeal to divers. This ship has come to be known as the "K.T.," from the only identifying marks found on the wreck. It is believed to have been a French minesweeper captured by the Germans and sunk by an Allied submarine near Sestri Levante, Liguria, during the Second World War. Lying at a depth of 183 feet, the wreck is accessible only to experienced divers.

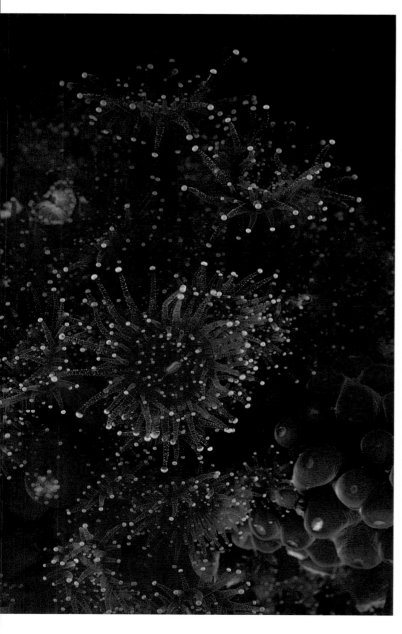

Over the nearly fifty years the ship has been under water, various forms of sea life, including anemones and sponges, have covered the twisted structures of the framework.

A School at the Bottom of the Sea

The *Rubis* (ruby) was a mine-laying submarine of the French Navy. Designed and built in 1925, it was the fourth in a series of vessels conceived for that specific duty; the others were the *Saphir* (sapphire), the *Turquoise*, the *Nautilus* (the only one not named for a precious stone), the *Diamant* (diamond), and the *Perle*. The *Rubis* spent its first three years of activity in and around Toulon. Then, in 1936, it was sent to Cherbourg to train submarine crews in the laying of mines.

Early in 1939, there was considerable fear of an outbreak of war, and the *Rubis* was brought back into the Mediterranean to Bizerte, in Tunisia, which was then a French colony. After a brief stay in Bizerte, the *Rubis* was attached to the Ninth Submarine Fleet based in Dundee, Scotland. It left that harbor on the night of May 3, 1940, and soon completed its first mission—the mining of the entrance to Egersund Fjord on the Norwegian coast. Then followed two more missions, in the same waters, at the conclusion of which the mining submarines were ordered to return home; the war was going very badly for France. They all returned except for the *Rubis*; its commander, Lt. Georges Cabanier, received orders to carry out one last mission—to mine the heart of Trondheim Fjord, where the German North Sea fleet had gathered.

Before departing, the commander asked to be informed as soon as possible should a cease-fire be signed. He was reassured that he would be notified, and he left on his final mission. Under Sub-Lieutenant Henri Rousselot's command, the *Rubis* first had to solve the problem of finding mines of suitable size. The correct armament was found, and the French submarine began to mine the fjord. The submarine was bombed (a near miss) and collided with a German submarine before returning home once again. The war ended for this brave vessel on June 23, 1940, when it entered (with its escort) the Algerian port of Oran, then a French territory. Only upon returning to Scotland did the crew learn that France had signed an armistice with Germany on June 22.

A monument to war heroism, this French submarine in the waters near Toulon is still serving its country today—as a sonar target for submarines. The Rubis, *honored for its distinguished service during the Second World War, has been intentionally saved from the scrapyard so that it can remain in its natural environment—precisely the waters from which it was originally launched. Before it was scuttled to be used as a sonar target, the ship was used as a floating school for submarine recruits. To better understand the historical importance of this submarine to the French Navy, it is useful to note that Admiral Georges Cabanier, one of the last commanders of the* Rubis, *ordered that his ashes be tossed into the sea at the exact location where his submarine is resting at a depth of 130 feet.*

The Rubis, *a mine-laying submarine, carried 32 mines and was equipped with 5 machine guns and 5 torpedoes. By the end of the Second World War, the submarine had laid 683 mines and sunk 14 ships and 7 torpedo-boat destroyers.*

THE PRIDE OF ITALY

Word of the tragedy was first broadcast on *RAI* radio news, on July 26, 1956. The following morning, the Italians rushed to buy newspapers, just as the Americans would the following day. The *Nuovo Corriere della Sera* carried this headline: "Italy has lost one of the finest ships of its mercantile navy—The *Andrea Doria* sinks in the Atlantic, rammed in the fog by a Swedish ship." An aerial photograph of the transatlantic liner, leaning on its side and already half submerged, was in the middle of the page.

A second article, by Dino Buzzati, was entitled "A Piece of our Homeland." It began in this way: "A bit of Italy has gone away with the terrifying speed of the sea disaster, and now it is lying in the deep grave of the ocean, with no known remedy." He ended the article with the word *addio*—farewell. The *Andrea Doria* still lies where it foundered, on a desolate tableland at a depth of 242 feet, 45 miles south-southeast of Nantucket Island.

The *Andrea Doria* had been laid on February 9, 1950, in the building slip of the Ansaldo Dockyards in Sestri Levante on behalf of the Società di Navigazione Italia. Launched on June 16, 1951, the ship had a tonnage of 29,100 tons and an overall length of 700 feet. The turbines gave it a maximum speed of 23 knots. It began service in January 1953 on the Genoa-Naples-New York route. A beautiful ship, it was a symbol of the economic miracle of Italy, which had had the courage to conceive and to complete it less than five years after the end of the Second World War.

For decades, the big transatlantic liners were the primary links to America from Europe and other parts of the world, but they were supplanted by the increase in air transportation. Those passengers who were on board the *Andrea Doria* for what was to become her last voyage were still nostalgic for the Atlantic crossing. They were the privileged few who could afford passage on a ship with three swimming pools, air-conditioning in every cabin, impeccable service, exquisite cuisine, and lively entertainment.

The powerful engines of the *Andrea Doria* were silenced forever on the night of July 25, 1956, only a few hours out from the sparkling lights of New York. Shortly after eleven that night, another, smaller liner—the *Stockholm*—collided with the *Andrea Doria* in heavy fog; the big left propeller was the last detail that could be made out before the hull disappeared under water. The bow struck the seabed and acted as a shock absorber, mitigating the crash to some extent. Fifty-four passengers, trapped in their cabins, injured, or unconscious, went down with the ship. A bitter controversy began immediately over which ship had struck the other, but to this day, it is not known which ship was at fault for the tragedy. Peter Gimbell, a documentary film maker and sport diver, was the first to see the *Andrea Doria* again. In 1976, he produced a documentary on the wreck.

In 1968, an Italian-American team arrived to dive on the wreck. They were Bruno Vailati, a world-famous documentary filmmaker; Stefano Carletti, a fisherman, scuba diver, sailor, and writer; and Al Giddings, a famous underwater photographer and inventor of a waterproof case for cameras. Assisting them on the expedition were Cosmo Dies (known as "Mimi") and Arnaldo Mattei. The five-man crew boarded the *Narragansett*, a tugboat that had been adapted for scientific expeditions, commanded by Jack Jacobsen. The result of the expedition was a film-length documentary entitled *Andrea Doria 74*, the same title Stefano Carletti chose for his book, published in December of the same year.

The threesome—Bruno Vailati with the movie camera, Al Giddings with the still camera, and Stefano Carletti with an explosive-head harpoon to deter the sharks—began the first of twenty-one dives on the wreck on July 6, 1968. In his book, Stefano Carletti describes the first dives: "After Al and Bruno have confirmed the presence of the wreck, we decide to go for a second dive. At 3:30 in the afternoon we enter the water; the low visibility and strong undercurrent are the same, and after a little difficulty in adjusting, I go down well. Bruno loses his knife during the dive and tries to catch it without success. Meanwhile Al overtakes me, and he and Bruno go ahead of me on the wreck; I arrive soon after. At a distance of no more than ten feet, I glimpse the left side of the *Andrea Doria* in the murky water. I reach the hull just below the boatdeck; I see the anchor our rope

The Andrea Doria *collided with a Swedish ship in heavy fog off Nantucket Island on July 25, 1956. Lying on the seabed at a depth of 242 feet, the ship, like the* Titanic, *has been the subject of numerous articles, books, and documentaries. In the years since the ship's sinking, underwater technology has become increasingly more sophisticated, enabling teams such as the one led by filmmaker Bruno Vailati in 1968 to explore and film the wreck for audiences across the world. There are many who feel that these wrecks should be left alone and that items found on the wrecks themselves and in the debris fields around them should remain in the sea.*

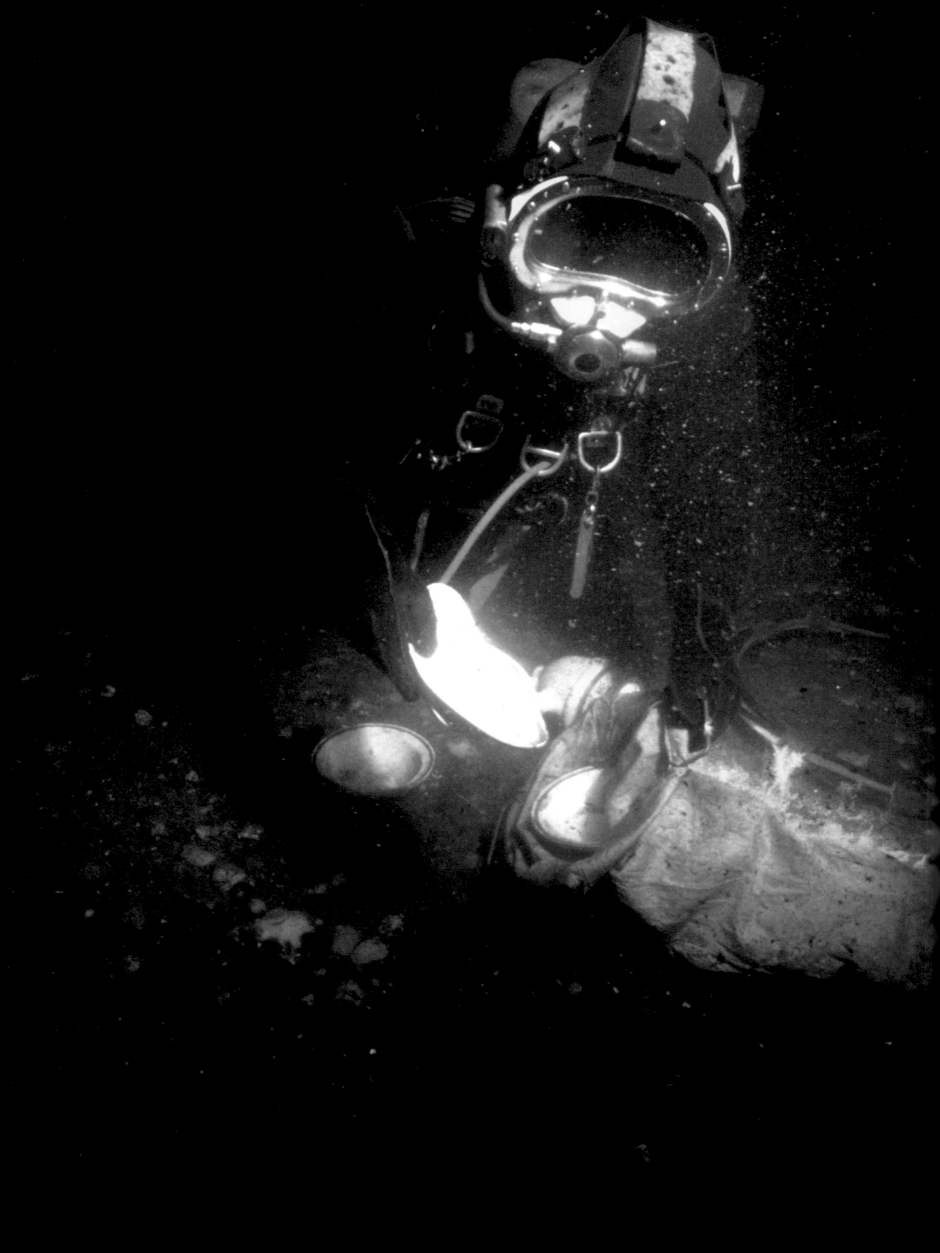

is tied to and then an even bigger one. Large fish are around us everywhere. My hands are numbed by the cold. I look around and see that our visibility is limited by giant fishes, and I wave to Bruno to notice them. But Bruno is thinking only about the shark. In spite of Mimi and Arnaldo's efforts, the protective cage with the explosive-head harpoon attached to it that was dipped into the sea during the first dive does not work as it should.

"Now I ask myself: what was the impression the wreck made on me? None—I was too worried about the dreadful environmental conditions—the darkness, the cold (in spite of special precautions such as a wetsuit, footgear, etc.). Last night before falling asleep, I thought about the ship. We should have felt pity for the injured (or dead?) colossus."

Stefano Carletti's diary describes in detail all dives on that expedition, including the last one, which ended at 12:03 P.M. on July 25 after a gradual, forty-minute return to the surface, spent, as usual, driving blue sharks away and looking back at the black hole of the seabed and ahead to the the milky light of the surface.

After the Vailati expedition, only one other diver—Peter Gimbel—returned to the wreck. He wanted to produce a second documentary on the *Andrea Doria*. In July of 1981, Gimbel and his team explored the wreck using a technique called "saturation diving," which enabled them to remain in the water up to eight hours at a time.

Gimbel recovered a Bank of Rome safe from the *Andrea Doria*, left it untouched for almost three years, and then, after much suspense, opened the safe on August 16, 1984, before television cameras. The safe, which had not remained water-tight, contained a few soggy bundles of 1,000-lire notes.

When he heard of the Gimbel recovery, Bruno Vailati wrote: "As for me, from a sentimental and emotional point of view, and considering that jealous feeling I seldom feel and much more seldom confess, it is right for the *Andrea Doria* to be lying where it is. Today it belongs to the sea; it has its own grim beauty, its reason for existence down there. It is no longer a man's work, it is a reef, one of the numerous reefs in the Atlantic and, in conclusion, I will not regret (in spite of all the ambitions I nourished toward the undertaking) if it should remain what it is—a reef lying on the seabed."

The Andrea Doria *was the pride of the Italian mercantile fleet, and all of Italy mourned the sinking of the magnificent ship that still carried passengers eager to experience "the Atlantic crossing" at a time when air travel was becoming increasingly more popular. One journalist, in writing about the sinking of the ship, characterized the* Andrea Doria *as "a bit of the best of Italy."*

COUSTEAU'S CONSHELF TWO

THE FUTURE OF MAN UNDER WATER

This metal hangar that housed the diving saucer, DS-2, is one of four buildings that made up the underwater village Conshelf Two, designed and built under the direction of Jacques Cousteau in 1963.

P ractically speaking, Capt. Jacques-Yves Cousteau was the inventor of the modern breathing apparatus, which has opened to man the conquest of the world under water. He built the apparatus in 1942 in occupied France, with engineer Emile Gagnar, improving upon the apparatus Navy Commander Le Prieur had built a few years earlier. Since that time, Cousteau has never ceased to be concerned with the sixth continent—the "world of silence."

Conshelf Two was an underwater "village" conceived and organized by Cousteau in order to conduct one of his remarkable experiments: a group of five men lived at the bottom of the sea

the experiment was Sha'ab Rumi, or "Roman Reef," near Port Sudan in the Red Sea, since it was the most suitable port near the coral reef that was to become the backdrop for the submarine village. Cousteau chose the Red Sea for its inhospitable conditions: if men could live submerged in those waters, they could live anywhere.

The four prefabricated steel buildings that made up the village were transported to the site by the *Rosaldo*, which served as Conshelf Two's "floating base." The building in which the five men lived was called "Starfish House"; it contained sleeping quarters, a kitchen, a laboratory, a darkroom, and the control center for the project, among other rooms. A "Saucer Hangar" was home to the *DS-2*, the project's diving saucer. The third building was a storehouse for tools. Fifty feet deeper was the "Deep Cabin," in which two divers would live for one week at ninety feet. To set up the village, divers from the *Calypso* worked for an entire month. In order to prevent the four buildings from bobbing to the surface like corks, lead bars were used to weigh them down.

The five men who occupied Conshelf Two for one month were treated to night after night of breathtaking views of undersea life from the safety of Starfish House. The divers adapted to their underwater quarters remarkably well, venturing forth to explore the reef or to take samples for scientific study. Manned undersea stations such as Conshelf Two will have many applications for the future; Cousteau is truly a pioneer whose work will pave the way for the future of man's life under water.

Cousteau's team lived for one month under water in the buildings of the village. After the project was completed, the village was dismantled, but the site, near Port Sudan, is still visited by divers and underwater photographers, who regard it as a kind of underwater ghost town.

for an entire month.

In September of 1962, Cousteau completed a pilot project, Conshelf One, in the Mediterranean: two men lived and worked in a single chamber for one week. In the early 1960s, this was all still in an experimental phase; Cousteau designed the second phase of the Conshelf program in 1963—the underwater village at Sha'ab Rumi.

After long and careful research by Albert Falco, the place selected for the logistical base of

PASSAGE INTO ANOTHER WORLD

The Red Sea, *Al Bahr Al Ahmar* in Arabic, the language spoken on most of its shores, is a sea of famous stories and of uninterrupted history. It is the Biblical sea, the sea that parted for the fleeing Jews and closed over the pursuing Pharaoh's army. It is the sea that washes the shores of Egypt, Sudan, and Ethiopia, and, on the opposite shore, Saudi Arabia and Yemen. It is the sea that connects the Indian Ocean with the Mediterranean. Surrounded by desert, by arid and barren lands tortured by the sun, the Red Sea, filling a tremendous wound in the Earth's crust, is deep, warm, and rich with underwater life. In this sea, the currents are weak, and the light from above is bright.

The only vein of passage for the traffic between ancient Mediterranean civilizations and those of Africa and Asia, the Red Sea, unlike the Mediterranean, did not experience a reduction of its cultural, strategic, or commercial importance as a result of the discovery of America. Heavy sea traffic such as that in the Red Sea always means numerous shipwrecks. But thanks to the physical characteristics of this sea, shipwrecks lying on the bottom present features rarely found elsewhere, even in other waters at the same latitude.

A ship sunk in cold waters, especially at a great depth, lies forever in the mystery of its shadows, its recesses difficult to reach, its rusting superstructures obliterated by layers of sea organisms; fish wander in and out like ghosts, in this "thing" that is, in any case, recognizable as manmade. But in the Red Sea, a wreck is something alive, an integral part of the underwater environment. Ships that sink in the Red Sea are smothered but also recreated by the chaotic and fantastic growth of corals.

A clear example of the extraordinary generative capacites of this sea is what can be considered a land wreck: the port of Suakin. Unlike Pompeii and Herculaneum, which were destroyed in one night by Vesuvius, Suakin, in Sudan, was slowly overtaken by the aggressive growth of the coral reefs. Eventually, access to the harbor was impossible; the sea bottom seemed to lift, and the town that had lived by the sea was suffocated.

Similar to Suakin are the shipwrecks in the Red Sea that have been drawn into the snare of its hidden reefs—some only several feet below water level. They remain there, permanently fixed to the surrounding coral.

But the most fascinating wrecks are under water. Many have been found, but only those accessible to experienced divers who have been diving for years in the Red Sea. The most ancient ships, those made of wood, have rotted away over the centuries, and their cargoes—amphorae, gold artifacts, ingots—have since been incorporated into the coral and lost forever. Most of the known wrecks, none more than a century old, are concentrated in the Strait of Gobal, at the extreme tip of the Sinai Peninsula. Here the depth does not exceed 130 feet, and this is the only passageway for ships sailing for the Suez Canal. This was not a problem for the small Egyptian ships or the Roman ones which, driven by oars, could maneuver with limited risk.

The problem began with the opening of the Suez Canal in 1869 and the resulting increase in the number of great steamers that rapidly ousted the great sailing ships—the legendary windjammers. These sailing ships, in order to reach their mother country, England, from India or Australia, had to round the Cape of Good Hope at the extreme tip of Africa and sail north through the Atlantic Ocean. The splendid clippers, with their reduced running costs as compared with the steamers, were irreplaceable over long distances and on open oceans. But having to negotiate the narrow passages of the Red Sea, they soon became obsolete and were forced to give way to mechanically-driven ships. Ports such as those at Bombay, Calcutta, Madras, and Karachi sadly witnessed the gradual disappearance of the majestic, tall-masted ships.

The Red Sea boasts the oldest and most complex role in the history of civilization of any body of water on Earth. And the many wrecks that populate the sea are very much alive; when a ship sinks in these waters, it becomes a host to a variety of underwater creatures and magnificent corals. Since the currents are weak, the water warm, and the light from the surface unusually bright, the environment around the wrecks is much like that of a greenhouse.

In the photograph above, a diver swims past one of the vehicles carried by the cargo boat Blue Belle, sunk in the mid-1970s at Sha'ab Su'adi in Sudan. Pictured to the right is the wreck of a cargo boat sunk along the Egyptian coast, near the Brothers Islands. On the following pages is the wreck of the Cedar Pride, a Lebanese mercantile ship.

THE *HAVEN*

A SUNKEN TANKER

 he white flag of Cyprus, with the island outlined in copper-yellow and two crossed olive branches in the center, waved proudly above the oil tanker *Haven*. But the ship blackened the sea and sky around it for days after it caught fire on April 11, 1991, and poured tons of crude oil into the Mediterranean. It happened a mile and a half off the coast of Italy, between Arenzano and Varazze. The thick black smoke obscured the sun from Arenzano nearly to Savona.

The ship, launched for the Troodos Shipping Company in 1973, had a displacement of 109,000 tons. Damaged in 1987 while in the Persian Gulf during the war between Iran and Iraq, the ship had been repaired and modernized in a shipyard in Singapore. It was the *Haven*'s second maiden voyage that ended in flames along the coast of Liguria.

The *Haven* was bound for the floating platform of Multedo, where it was scheduled to pump the bulk of its crude oil into a pipeline linked to depots on land. But an explosion occurred on board the ship during a routine procedure. Recalling the accident, Donatos Lilis, first mate, said: "We had unloaded 80,000 tons and we wanted to carry the remaining crude oil in a single hold: it is a standard operation. We were using a pump to move the crude oil from the two side holds to the central one when I heard a very loud noise. It was an iron bar beating against another, causing sparks. Perhaps a pump cover had broken. Then there was the terrible blast." Five crewmen, including the captain, lost their lives in the disaster.

For three days and nights, the thick smoke, the high flames, and the explosions transformed that stretch of coastline into an inferno and the entire area into an ecological nightmare. The cleanup operation involved hundreds of men on dozens of ships, working frantically to contain the fire and the oil spill by discharging broadsides of water with their water cannons and placing miles of inflatable barriers around the big oil stains. Much of the oil spilled from the burning tanker was consumed in flames. In a second stroke of luck, tar and oil were kept from the Italian coastline by winds and currents.

After a day of fire, the bow of the ship went under. The hull was expected to break in two, resulting in an uncontrollable loss of crude oil. A major ecological disaster would seriously threaten the livelihood of tourist resorts on the Italian and French Rivieras. Luckily, when the *Haven* sank on Sunday morning, April 14, the entire hull went down on a flat and sandy seabed, skimming but not penetrating a rocky spur. Soon after the sinking, an ROV (Remote-Operated Vehicle) able to broadcast images of the hull and the surrounding seabed visited the wreck and confirmed that the hull was intact.

The Mediterranean is a small inland sea, and around it there are ten countries, among them some of the most industrialized in the world; along its miles of coastline are 200,000 inhabitants, most concentrated in 120 coastal towns. In the summer months, 100 million tourists pour into the area. The Mediterranean supports one-sixth of all the maritime traffic in the world, with a daily transit of 600 ships. The *Haven*'s sinking did not cause as much damage to the Mediterranean environment as had been feared at first. But lying motionless on the seabed, the ship serves as a warning of the potential for disaster caused by these huge tankers that transport tons of oil across our waterways.

The thick, black smoke from the burning oil tanker could be seen for miles along the Italian coast. Attempts to extinguish the fire lasted for three days and nights until, on the morning of April 14, the ship finally sank. The wreck now lies on the seabed as an ominous reminder of the potential for disaster these huge tankers carry with them.

PHOTO CREDITS

A group of eels emerges from the twisted plates of a wreck off the Mediterranean coast of France.